# PROVISIONING—BOWSPRIT TO TRANSOM

*Dottie Haynes*

*Text Contribution, Illustrations and Photography*

*Gene Haynes*

*The  Complete Guide to Becoming a Bluewater First Rate First Mate*
*… The First Time Out!*

*GOLDBERRY PUBLISHING*
*Rte 2 Box 3028*
*Lopez WA 98261*

*Library of Congress Catalog Number: 94-96221*

*ISBN 0-9641312-2-6*

*Cover design by Teutschel Design Services, Palo Alto CA 94306*

*Cover photograph, "Whither Thou at Close Haul," and page 36 by Miles Ringle, Berkeley CA 94705*

# *TABLE OF CONTENTS*

## LIST OF ILLUSTRATIONS

*To Gene … a man with mana*

*The Best Skipper—Husband—Friend—Teammate—Lover*

*Bar none*

*"…Until one is committed there is hesitancy, the chance to draw back, always ineffectiveness. Concerning all acts of initiative (and creation), there is one elementary truth, the ignorance of which kills countless ideas and splendid plans:* **that the moment one definitely commits oneself, then Providence moves too.** *All sorts of things occur to help one that would never otherwise have occurred. A whole stream of events issues from the decision, raising in one's favour all manner of unforeseen incidents and meetings and material assistance, which no man could have dreamt would have come his way. I have learned a deep respect for one of Goethe's couplets:*

**"'Whatever you can do, or
dream you can, begin it.**

**"'Boldness has genius,
power and magic in it.'"**

**— W. H. Murray**

### *HOW DO I SAY THANKS TO SUCH AS THESE???*

The encouragement and support of others has been boundless and without them, no completed product would have seen the light of day. Those others consist of Sheryn Hara, Hara & Company, Lynnwood, WA, my publicist and marketing specialist, who took on this project with such enthusiasm; Susi Henderson, Infinity Publishing Services, Lynnwood, WA, who went from disk to paper to disk, no easy task. Along with my computer guru, Peter Cooper, One Stop Computers, Anacortes, WA, they won the battle of outdated software and seemingly incompatible hardware. Thanks too, to Sara and Dennis Teutschel, Teutschel Design Services, Palo Alto, CA for the cover design; and of course Vicki McCown, Anacortes, WA, who proofread through the pages and cleaned up the infamous inconsistencies. My heartfelt thanks, gratitude and love to all, team.

In addition, efforts of more than one person have gone into the actual creation of ***Provisioning—Bowsprit to Transom.*** As in the actual sailing (even single-handed sailing as Gene will be the first to agree), no one can do it alone. Therefore, for loving efforts beyond the call of duty, profound thanks and gratitude go to:

…David Stewart, D.D.C, whom you will meet in Chapter 10, "…And Healthy." David, who is not only our chiropractor but a dear friend and fellow sailor as well, greatly assisted Gene in his single-handed race by outfitting him with medical gear and supplies. When I asked David to write down what had been included, he did so willingly, and as I state at the onset of Chapter 10, he also gave me verbal permission to edit as I saw fit. Editing was not necessary, but I did add an addendum or two. Forgive, David!

… Pete and Liz Lismer, friends first, boating neighbors and former yacht club cronies as added assets, I thank them for proofreading the sailing terminology in Chapter 2. I asked for their expertise to help determine: Is it accurate?

… My beloved and lovely daughter, Karen: a first mate in her own right and hopefully typical of the reader of ***Provisioning—Bowsprit to Transom,*** for proofreading the same segment, but from a different tack: Does it make sense?

… And of course, to my beloved Gene, the strongest and most loyal member of my support team, for so many reasons: for permission to use his preparation article (first published in *Cruising World* magazine) which forms the basis of Chapter 3, "You and Your Boat as a Whole," and which is directed to the skipper; for allowing his other previously published articles to be incorporated into Appendix E; for verifying the material given the Lismers and Karen, adding his tips and gentle memory joggers. It goes without saying my thanks and appreciation are wrapped up in a whole lot of love.

## TRADEMARK ACKNOWLEDGMENTS

All possible efforts have been made to acknowledge the specific products and give correct trademark credit to the manufacturers. Some products, however, are not names on the official U.S. Trademark Association listing, used as the sole guideline for this publication. Therefore, for those products not named, it is assumed the product has at least been copyrighted; we have thus acknowledged this as such in the body of the book Shown below, these products are referenced as "a product of" to the manufacturer and/or distributor of same, rather than "a registered trademark of."

**Ace**® elastic bandages is a registered trademark of Bectin Dickenson and Co., Franklin Lakes NY 07417-1883; **Alka-Seltzer**® antacid analgesic tablets and **Bactine**® wound sterilizer are registered trademarks of Miles Inc., Consumer Health Line Division, Elkhurst IN 46515; **Anderson Pea Soup©, Snow's Chowder©** and **Soup Starters©** are products of Borden Inc., Columbus OH 43215; **Ben Gay**® analgesic ointment and **Bonine**® motion sickness preparation are registered trademarks of Leeming Division of Pfizer Inc., New York 10017; **Bisquick**® baking mix is the registered trademark of General Mills, Minneapolis MN 55440; **Bullfrog©** sunscreen is a product of Chattem Inc., Chattanooga TN 37409; **Carnation instant hot chocolate©** mix is a product of Carnation Co., Los Angeles CA 90036; **Cream of Wheat**® cereal is a registered trademark of Nabisco Products, Passaic NJ 07055; **D.A.G. Solution©** is a product of Meyers Distributing Co., Upland CA 91786; **Dermicel©** adhesive is a product of Johnson and Johnson, New Brunswick NJ 08963-2400; **Di-Gel**® antacid tablets is a registered trademark of Plough Inc., Memphis TN 38151; **Dramamine**® motion sickness preparation is a registered trademark of Richardson-Vicks Inc., Shelton CT 06484; **Dream Whip**® dessert topping is a registered trademark of Kraft Products, White Plains NY 10626; **Foille©** ointment is a product of Blistex Inc., Oakbrook IL 60521; **Handi-Wrap II**® plastic film is the registered trademark of Dow Chemical Co., sold by Dow Consumer Products, Indianapolis IN 46268-05411; **Imodium A-D**® anti-diarrheal medication is the registered trademark distributed by McNeilab Inc., Ft. Washington PA 19034; **Jiffy Pop**® popcorn is a registered trademark of American Home Foods, Inc., New York 10017; **Joy©** detergent is a product of Proctor and Gamble, Cincinnati OH 45202; **Kaopectate**® anti-diarrheal medicine is a registered trademark of The Upjohn Co., Kalamazoo MI 49001; **Kikkoman©** Sauce(s) are products of K Foods Inc., Walworth WI 53184; **Kitchen Bouquet©**, food coloring agent, is a product of The HVR Co., Oakland Ca 94612; **Krusteaz©** pancake flour is a product of Continental Mills Inc., Kent WA 98032-1198; **Metamucil**® laxative is a registered trademark of Proctor and Gamble, Cincinnati OH 45202; **Nestle Quik**® instant hot chocolate mix is a registered trademark of Nestle Food Corp., Baltimore MD 21227; **NoDoz**® drowsiness relief tablets is a registered trademark of Bristol-Meyers, Evansville IN 47721; **Pam**® Vegetable Spray is a product of Boyle-Midway Household Products, New York 10017; **Q-Tips**® cotton swabs is a registered trademark of Cheeseborough-Pond's Inc., Greenwich CT 06830; **Rye-Krisp**® crackers is a registered trademark of Ralston Purina Co., St. Louis MO 63164; **Shake 'n Bake**® coating mixes is a registered trademark and **Tang©** is a product of Kraft General Foods Corp., White Plains NY 10625; **Latitude 38** sailing magazine is published by Latitude 38, Sausalito CA 94966; **Soft Scrub**® cleansing agent is a registered trademark of Clorox Co., Oakland, CA 94612; **Top Ramen**® Soups is a registered trademark of Nissen Foods, Gardena CA; **Tupperware**® food storage containers is a registered trademark of Tupperware Products, Orlando FL 32802; **Velcro**® hook and loop fasteners is a registered trademark of Velcro USA Inc., Manchester NH 03108; **V-8**® Juice is a registered trademark of Campbell Soup Company, Camden NJ 08103; **Wondra Flour**® is the registered trademark of General Mills, Minneapolis MN 55440; **Wyler's**® instant lemonade mix is a registered trademark of Thomas J. Lipton, Inc., Englewood Cliffs NJ 07632; **Ziploc**® resealable plastic bags is the registered trademark of Dow Chemical Co., sold by Dow Consumer Products, Indianapolis IN 46268-0511.

The sea never changes and its works, for all the talk of men, are wrapped in mystery.

— Joseph Conrad

# *NOTE*

I don't mean to be sexist, God forbid, but since the majority of First Mates are of the female gender and the term "Captain" when capitalized is still treated as a male pronoun, this is the tone applied to what you are about to read, but done, gentle reader, in the name of simplicity only.

My apologies in advance to those able and competent female skippers of their own vessels, some of whom I have had the privilege of knowing personally. These include once local San Francisco skippers such as Linda Newland: single-handed skipper San Francisco/Hawaii at least twice that I know of, San Francisco to Japan on a separate voyage ... a mere sampling of the accomplishments that number among so many other of her notable traits. Then there is petite Amy Boyer, single-handed skipper of her 21' craft, again San Francisco/Hawaii (first woman to finish), not to mention the Mini TransAt from the Canary Islands to Aruba. On that voyage, her craft hit or was hit—she thought by a whale—causing her to turn back for repairs. She *still* managed to be the first woman to finish. I forget which of these voyages she was on that she celebrated her 21st birthday. Alone, but doing her thing.

These names come to mind without too much effort, along with the likes of Naomi James, about whom I have read and admired in the early archives of learning. And of late, all those ladies whose names currently grace the pages of the popular sailing magazines.

I have also had the pleasure to knowing, admiring, and trading galley tips with those competent men who have elected to rule the galley in the craft of their choice, skippered by the Captains of their choice.

To these personal friends and to their counterparts all over the world, I bow in apology. But as stated, for simplicity's sake, mates, it's "she" and "he" in the now antiquated nomenclature.

So sue me.

And in his Christmas stocking, hung by the mast with care, may every Captain afloat be decorously awarded the Captain Hook Award and a "Don't Shout At Me!" tee-shirt from the First Mate of The Craft when, to his sorrow, he: shouts/yells/screams/curses ... just once too many times. I guarantee it: he will!

*"Whatever women do, they must do it twice as well as men to be thought half as good. Luckily, this is not difficult."*

— *Charlotte Whitton, June 1963*

# 1

## *WHAT'S IT ALL ABOUT?*

### *The Book*

### *The Author*

*"Because it's there."*                    — *G. H. Mallory,* **The Ascent of Everest**

A s the title indicates, **BOWSPRIT TO TRANSOM** is dedicated to and geared toward those First Mates helping to ready, or soon to be readying, themselves and their vessel for serious extended bluewater cruising. This is contrary to the more numerous day-sailors who have no plans to leave familiar waters, and who sail primarily on weekends, with permanent homes and priority interests elsewhere.

A seagoing vessel, again contrary to the "day-sailor" category, and regardless of its size, must be a self-contained unit. Therefore, pre-planning is vital: for comfort, for safety and for sanity (not necessarily in that order!) To accomplish this for extended passages is awesome enough for a seasoned first mate to contemplate. But Good Lord, what about the *pioneering* first mate, on her first time major undertaking? Is it panic time?

No. It's Challenge Time.

*PROVISIONING—BOWSPRIT TO TRANSOM* tackles this tendency to panic, even though what lies ahead may be the maiden bluewater voyage for both crew and vessel.

If you apply the tips, hints and suggestions within these pages, you will learn, among other things:

- Coping with seasickness… What to have on board to offset, what supplies to keep on hand for the crew when the cook just can't, and how to help it come to an end.

- Getting your feet wet… Some preliminary tips for getting you and your craft ready, while still in controlled situations and in comfortable familiar waters. Included is a review and run-down of the so important sailin' lingo (not the basics: you already know "below" from "downstairs," for cryin' out loud), but taking a sensible look at some words and phrases you may not have had to deal with as yet.

- Reviewing both your boat as a whole (from the Skipper's point of view as well as that of the First Mate), and taking a look at cabin appointments: what to consider and what is best left ashore.

- <u>Personal gear</u>… what to include and what to leave behind.

- <u>Safety tips</u> for belowdecks are discussed, and finally…

- Getting down to brass tacks… How to store, function and cope with ease in your ship's galley. <u>Maxi use in a Mini space</u>… No matter how compact your craft, *you have more space than you think you do!* Find and utilize that extra space to the fullest.

- <u>How to pre-plan</u>. The main key to a successful total offshore experience with your complete uncluttered self-contained unit at sea.

- How to <u>plan actual workable menus,</u> using supplies and provisions that work, learned through first-hand experience, including suggestions for those first few days out as the boat and crew adjust to each other. Included are <u>two weeks worth of menus,</u> as well as real and <u>workable recipes,</u> to be used verbatim or as building blocks, so you and your crew can eat well…while cruising or racing, in safety and in relative comfort.

- Provisions and supplies <u>that work</u>, with practical suggestions for stowage of all…and

- Supplies, provisions and equipment that <u>don't work</u>. A few of the familiar but landlocked equipment to remain behind. You won't need them.

- <u>Clean…crew and boat</u>. Supplies and gear: What is needed and what is not.

- Provisioning your self-contained unit also means learning some <u>health tips</u>; you will find within these pages suggestions for medical supplies as well as suggested reference material to supplement your ship's medical library.

- Your off-hours need not be all work, y'know. How to set up an evening of birthday fun, or quiet romance...included here in the pre-planning for the sailing experience ahead.

Much more is here: How to work with the Captain of your choice in dividing up the responsibility, who is in charge of what, how you as the First Mate can help, out of the galley as well as in; even some off-the-cuff suggestions from my Captain to yours.

There is room for only one Captain on any vessel. Be sure in your own mind there is no doubt as to who that Captain is…but here are some sneaky suggestions on what to do when he yells at you once too often…and believe me, he will!

### *THE AUTHOR*

No round-the-world-sailor I, nor the most experienced in the number of nautical miles under my personal keel. Rather, practical experience comes to play in having lived aboard our 33 ft. sloop "Whither Thou," with the Captain of my choice named Gene, full time for ten years, and loving every minute of it. (Well, almost every minute. There was a time, on our return passage from British Columbia to California, that was a bit more wet and adventurous than we planned!)

…Experience is here in having had the responsibility given me to provision that same 33' sloop for my 50-plus husband's singlehanded race San Francisco to Kauai, Hawaii (try watching your adored husband *and home* sail under the Golden Gate Bridge as you go back to your car with the thudding and empty reality: *Whereinell do I go now*??)

…Experience in re-supplying said craft for the return trip Kauai to San Francisco which I helped sail and crew. Thirty-three gorgeous days alone. Gene paid dearly for those eighteen days of racing by himself!

…Experience in repeating the provisioning responsibility and scenario, this time for a 53' ketch on her virgin voyage to Canada with a crew of nine (and I do mean "virgin": not a salt or pepper shaker in sight). In charge of that same galley while in Canadian waters with the vessel's conglomerate owners and guests throughout the summer; then the return trip to California with a brand new crew of five.

…The same vessel and galley, but this time in absentia: provisioning for an all-male racing crew of seven—again, San Francisco to Kauai.

All that experience took coordination and planning. Lots of planning. And yes… moments of panic, especially for one who prior to "Whither Thou" and Gene, had never set foot on anything smaller than the "Stella Solaris"…one who, just barely on the sunny side of 50, was fresh over a 38-year habit of a pack+ of smokes per day…one who had then (and still has) claustrophobia. My fear of heights was nothing to write home about either. (Guess who gets to go to the top of our 40' mast for minor repairs? You've got it, sport). Would you believe: I never did learn to swim; I have an unholy terror of the water. But the terror is *in* it. Not *on* it.

So much for advantages of youth, past experiences or prior lifestyles. Did I tell you? I am also a grandmother, and was when this whole new lifestyle began. One magazine called me the "Urban Grandmother Turned First Mate." Really.

So what **is** the nitty of the gritty? Just this: Forget the past! It is **the present,** it is **the future** that counts.

You know more than you think you do, so relax and trust your own instincts and the common horse sense you were born with and have always relied on.

No one was born an accomplished sailor, you know. Not me, not you, not Linda or Amy…not even those racing mavens who compete in such events as the America's Cup, come to think of it.

Toward the present and the future then, dear reader: This book's for you.

Enjoy.

*"The past is the present, isn't it? It's the future too."*                         — Eugene O'Neill

# 2

## GETTING YOUR FEET WET

*You Know More Than You Think You Do!*

*First You Get Seasick…*

*…Then You Get Better!*

*…And Smarter: Sailing Lingo Made Easy*

*Out Of The Galley*

**"No one knows what he can do until he tries."**                        — *P. Syrus*

**Y**ou know more than you think you do! Think about it: after all, you have been around that boat and the Skipper of your choice for some time now. You have both decided the time has come to fish or cut bait: Why *not* put this landlubber life on hold for awhile? Head out…and this time, keep on going.

Are you ready? Sure you're ready. But, it does persist, doesn't it—that uneasy feeling: Can I do it?… Am I up to it? Damn! There is so much to learn!

Sure you can. Yes, you *are* up to it. You are forgetting what you have already absorbed up to now: physical fitness, running a home, financial abilities and positive relationships with family, friends and business cohorts. Add to these plusses the positives of intellectual curiosity and a spirit of adventure which got you here (by choice, remember) in the first place.

Whether you live aboard (as Gene and I did for ten years) or enjoy on-again, off-again long distance cruising, or both, life aboard ship takes a shift of priorities. There is a difference, a **big** difference:  between *chore* and *challenge*, between *doing without* and *returning to basics*, between *inconvenience* and *discovering your pioneering spunk.*

The differences are all in attitudes and priorities. You don't need them: every electrical plug-in convenience invented, or having hot steaming water at the drop of a faucet. Instead, it is time to adopt the sea and all her ways, along with gaining a growing healthy respect for her power and knowing that she is now, and always will be, in total command.

But mostly, it takes your commitment to one Captain and one boat, in that order. As, conversely, that Captain and that boat must commit themselves to you.

*"How many things I can do without!"*                              — *Socrates*

I cannot stress enough the importance of the relationship between you and the Skipper of your choice. There is room for only one Captain on a boat. Put away your ideas of total equality, mate. He and he alone has the final say for the safety of the crew and the vessel. When he gives an order, carry it out and carry it out **now**. Question the wisdom later if you must, when you are out of the frenetic situation and calm has been restored.

Being a First Mate means accepting the status that is one mini-step down the ladder in the chain of command. This is as it must be, albeit a challenge to accept. When you are at sea, that sea is always in command; she will never be conquered. To accept this reality is sailing with prudence; anyone who thinks and acts otherwise is a fool. Man will ever be the guest, to come and go at the sea's discretion and decree. When the sea becomes less than hospitable, every second counts, to keep the vessel afloat and the crew safe. This requires immediate and instant reaction to every command the captain issues. Act now, question later, and never, **never** forget: one Captain, one Captain only.

No matter what the size of the vessel, there are two nerve centers on board: the nav station and the galley. The Skipper usually takes care of the first one, although the First Mate may elect to help with the vital time checks and subsequent math required. The First Mate usually takes care of the second, although the Skipper will no doubt do his share of cooking and cleaning up en route.

Both nerve centers must be maintained at top efficiency. ***Neither is more or less important than the other.*** Therefore, you as the First Mate are just as vital to the well-being of the ship as is the Skipper. As you operate side by side, you create a three way team: Skipper, First Mate, and your worthy craft, a man-made creation that can only *obey* commands, not instigate them.

*"Man marks the earth with ruin—his control stops with the shore."*     **— Lord Byron**

### FIRST YOU GET SEASICK...

**"Oh the wild joys of living!"**                                    **— Robert Browning**

Now is the time to cut your sailing baby teeth and test your growing bluewater abilities. So you don't get seasick in the confines of local day sailing waters: this does not mean *mal de mer* isn't waiting for you out there. Seasickness is simply one more item on your cope list. Believe it, it will be dealt with eventually by *somebody* on board, so avoid the mistake of ignoring that it exists. Talk to your doctor. Ask about the ear patches containing Scopolamine, the strongest motion sickness reliever known.

Motion sickness is a result of a lack of communication between the brain and the inner ear. The ear patches help by taking the relief straight to the source by process of osmosis, as your skin absorbs the active medication.

> (<u>CAUTION</u>: Do not use for more than three days. By this time, seasickness normally begins to subside anyway. If not in three days, it will soon. Keeping the patches on longer, or applying a new one, will only lead to problems).

> (<u>CAUTION</u>: These patches should be applied the night before departure. After application, do not drink any alcohol: the two do not mix.)

> See Chapter 10, "...And Healthy" for further comments on motion sickness.

When and if it hits, use the "First Bumpy Days" suggestions described in Chapter 8, "The Real and Workable Galley/Menu Planning Summary," and Appendix A, "Menus Tried and True," to see you through.

I promise, guys, those upheavals in your system **will** end, and at the end of those first rough days, you will be ravenous and rarin' to go!!

**...*THEN YOU GET BETTER!***

**"Slow and steady wins the race."**                  **— Aesop, The Tortoise and The Hare**

Y ou and the rolling seas have come to terms and the queasies are over. Next step: time to test your piloting abilities.

Can you stand a four-on-four-off watch if the crew is just the two of you? Can you stand any length of watch at all, knowing the good Captain needs his sleep too, and *you* may have to make fast and competent decisions? Can you read the tides? Or will you, like yours truly first time out the Golden Gate, circle the same spot of ocean for four solid hours? I thought that damn lighthouse would never retreat to aft.

Chapter 3 begins in-depth study of major readying tips and suggestions. Towards this first preliminary gearing-up, though, plan a new conduit of energy. Begin ***now*** to modify your outlook and priorities: from primarily weekend fun-type sailing to the next rung on the ladder of learning groundwork.

The goal from here on in is to begin preparing you and your craft for the adventure ahead. In this vein then: While still in controlled waters and situations, and keeping within your current range and scope of knowledge and energy, consider these suggested areas for planning and testing:

*TIP: Write down and keep for reference the results of the testing.*

With your Captain:

- Try out every combination of sail configurations your sail complement will allow; do it in frisky weather to find out the boat's reactions.

- Plan at least one 24-hour sail-around of your familiar waters, incorporating watch and duty assignments.

- Set up every conceivable controlled situation you can think of to check out reactions and responses from yourselves and your boat.

- Discuss, discard, experiment.

- Check all equipment in all kinds of weather, deliberately sailing in foul weather *as well as at night* during your sail-around.

- Plan an actual "man overboard" to see what it really takes to get back aboard. Better here than at sea, sport fans.

- Seriously consider taking courses from the local U.S. Coast Guard Auxiliary. They have excellent ones in general seamanship, coastal and inland water navigation. The hours are "doable" and they are excellent tools to help build your preliminary learning platforms.

*TIP: With regard to navigation, <u>please</u> do not leave this completely to the Captain. Even if you personally don't plan to take sextant shots or man the SatNav or Loran, it is mighty helpful to have a general idea of what is involved. A course in Celestial Navigation from a local college is a big help, and they supplement those Coast Guard courses referred to above.*

*TIP: If you value the relationship, I do not recommend trying to learn navigation from your Captain, no matter how good he is. Rather the same as trying to learn how to drive from your husband. Need I say more?*

- Test the life system at your authorized inspection center.

You don't have a life system? Get one. NOW. Do not wait until just before departure, it takes time to find out what it will do, *and what it won't.* Go to the inspection center; they will have a life system open for review, they will assist you to understand your own version. Ask pointed questions: How <u>do</u> two people actually board the darn thing?

Once you know its limitations of space and capability, pack the life system with the supplies *you* will need, not necessarily what the brochure says you ought to need, although do pay attention to their suggestions. Some tips to consider: extra eye glasses, extra supplies of personal medications, extra caps and gloves. Look into a solar distillation kit that converts salt water to fresh. Pack simple fishing gear, freeze-dried rations that can be eaten as-is, and high energy foods; e.g., hard candy, granola bars, trail mix without chocolate that melts, all kinds of nuts, etc.

A life system is costly. Like a parachute, it will be the one piece of equipment you spend major bucks for that you pray to God you will never have to use. But don't go to sea without it or without knowing how to properly use it to **its** fullest capability and **your** fullest understanding.

- Sail *every single opportunity* you have or can create, in *all kinds of weather.*

- Sail with any crew you plan to take to sea.

- Sail shorthanded.

- Well before departure, each of you do a singlehanded stint, again in controlled waters with a controlled situation.

Every time you sail, every experiment you try, every testing you subject youself and the vessel to gives *you* that much more confidence, increases your experience...and, gives you a greater itch to **GO**!

*... AND SMARTER!*

**"Training is everything. The peach was once a bitter almond; cauliflower is nothing but a cabbage with a college education."**
                                                                **— Mark Twain**

N ot by any means lastly, your learning will include patience, both with the sea and with each other. Patience and Learning. Part of this means: *please* learn the correct terminology. Boy, I sure hope *you* are not as green as this kid was, calling the jib sheet a "dumb snarly rope." Do you have any idea how many "ropes" there are on a boat? Try **that** when the weather is at its worst, your vessel is at a 40° heel and your Captain is screaming "WHAT SON OF A SEA COOK ##@$%!!! GEEDEE ROPE???"

Incidentally, how many ropes *are* there on a boat? Answer: None. "Rope" is a landlubber term meaning "line," and each line has its own nomenclature...named for the sail to which it is either attached, for that sail's particular function, or incorporating the age-old tradition of the nautical vocabulary...a colorful, historic and universal one.

You, dear reader, know this already, along with the basics: "Topside" isn't "up-stairs," fore 'n' aft is just that. It's "galley," "head," "sole" and "companionway," not staircase. But specific nautical terms, used to describe parts of the vessel, to simplify commands and responses when handling gear, or to recognize passing vessels...these are also helpful in making life both more pleasant and less complicated for you and the Skipper. Therefore, gentle person, what follows are some terms to be aware of right from the onset, but which you may not have had the opportunity to come to grips with. Yet.

I have also deliberately avoided most of those connected with navigation; you will learn those terms in conjunction with sharpening your navigational skills. (Whoops! There are exceptions: "Latitude," "longitude," "meridian," "sight" and "variation" are included here, but for easy reference only.)

I could put all of this at the end of the book as others have done, entitle it "Glossary" to be forever out mind and never referred to again. I could, but I won't. Learning the lingo is far more important than most people admit, so wade through this on the way to the rest of the book. It's shallow wading, folks...barely getting your feet wet.

*SAILING LINGO MADE EASY*

*"Get your facts first, then you can distort them as much as you please."* **— Mark Twain**

| | |
|---|---|
| **afterguy** | The line controlling the fore/aft trim of the spinnaker pole. |
| **aloft** | Above. Up the mast or in the rigging, as in…The <u>Captain</u> is aloft. |
| **apparent wind** | Combination of the true wind and that which is developed by the boat speed and direction. |
| **athwart(ships)** | Across. Opposite of fore and aft. |
| **backstay** | Wire mast support leading from the top of the mast to the stern. Prevents the mast from falling forward. |
| **backwind** | 1) Wind deflected from a forward sail onto the one behind; |
| | 2) When the jib is on port but the wind is from starboard. |
| **ballast** | Something heavy—usually lead—placed in (or on) the keel for stability. Can be the keel itself; it can even be water. |
| **battens** | Stiffening boards to support the sail shape. See reference under "roach." |
| **beam reach** | Wind at right angles to the boat; also one of the fastest points of sail. Great sailing! |
| **bear away/bear off** | See "fall off." |
| **beat/beating** | Tacking to windward, sailing hard on the wind. Exhausting sailing if done for a long period of time. |

**bight**
A bend or loop in a line.

**binnacle**
Freestanding compass casing.

**bitter-end**
The extreme end of a line. Extreme end of patience too, at times!

**block**
A pulley.

**blooper**
Similar to a spinnaker, but whereas the spinnaker has both clew and tack free to be maneuvered, the blooper has one of the two fastened to the base of the forestay.

**bobstay**
A chain, wire or rod positioned from the bow to the end of the bowsprit. Supports against upward pull of the headstay.

**bowline(knot)**

1   2   3

Pronounced "b-o-l-i-n," this is <u>the</u> most important knot to learn. Forms a loop that will not slide or jam. Practice until you can do it blindfolded. Literally!

*TIP: There is a way to remember, something about "the rabbit goes AROUND THE TREE..." Effective but not particularly professional. Learn the knot without the nursery rhyme.*

**bowsprit**
Spar on which the jib may be set. Projects horizontally from the bow.

**brightwork**
Well-kept varnished woodwork and that inevitable brass. Your job most of the time.

**broach**
Uncontrolled rounding up of a boat which is overpowered and knocked down while reaching or running. Do not **DO** this! It will louse up your whole day.

**broad reach**
Any heading between a beam reach and a run. Sailing with the wind aft of abeam.

**bulkhead**  More than a partition, it holds the shell of the vessel to its designed shape under extreme sailing stress. The design, along with the chain plate, determines the vessel's ***true integrity.***

**bulwarks**  Raised part of the deck usually following the sheer line, for protection of crew and gear.

**bumpkin**  A spar projecting horizontally from the stern, to which a permanent backstay or mizzen sheet is attached.

**bunkboard**  A bulwark (wood or cloth) to keep the off-watch crew snug in their bunk during heavy rolling seas. Also called a "leeboard."

**burden boat**  When on a collision course the vessel that is responsible for giving way. Example: Port tack gives way to a starboard tack, downwind gives way to any tack.

*A good idea is to read up on marine right-of-way.*

*Goes without saying, freighters don't count: They are NEVER the burden boat!*

**cam cleat**  A ***spring-loaded*** clamping device for securing lines. See "jam" cleat.

**carriage**  The sliding car (traveler) on a track, to which a sheet or vang is attached.

**cast(to)**  Take a sounding with the lead, pronounced "led."

**cavitation**  The vessel is "spinning its wheels" because the propeller, rotating faster than it should, has created a body of bubbles and has nothing to grab onto. Rather like a car stuck in a rut and…spinning its wheels.

**center of effort**  The point at which the sum total of sail forces is applied.

| | |
|---|---|
| **centerboard** | The vertical plate or board lowered through a slot in the keel of a shallow draft vessel to provide lateral resistance. Many small racing vessels use this as the actual keel. |
| **chain plate** | A metal strap on the side of the vessel to which the lower end of the shroud is fastened. ***Integrity most vital*** since it keeps the mast from falling down sideways. |
| **chine** | In a deep bottom boat, this is the junction between the bottom and topsides. Sometimes sharp and distinct, sometimes not. |
| **chock** | Wooden or metal blocks which act as pads and are cut and shaped to hold anchor, spinnaker pole, etc., securely in place. |
| **cleat** | A fitting used to secure a line.<br><br>*Keep in mind that the cleats located on the docks can and should be used to provide mechanical advantage. If you loop the bow or stern line immediately around the dock cleat, even a featherweight mate can keep that vessel in line.* |
| **clevis pin** | A pin to secure rigging to a turnbuckle, mast tang, chain plate, etc.; secured in place by a cotter pin instead of a nut. |
| **clew** | The point on a sail where the leech and foot meet. |
| **close hauled** | Sailing as close into the wind as you can get; sails are trimmed practically fore and aft. Can be uncomfortable sailing. |
| **clove hitch** | The knot securing a line at right angles around a post. |
| **coaming** | The side of the cabin extending above deck level. |

**cook strap**          A safety line which keeps the cook upright and in relative safety to prepare meals while underway in rotten seas. If no strap is available, have the skipper lean on the opposite side from the galley and you lean on him. (Not so far-fetched as it sounds; worked for us on many occasions.)

**cotter pin**          A small metal pin used to keep a clevis pin in place or a nut from working loose.

**cringle**          An eye on the outside of a sail fitted with a metal thimble.

**cunningham**          Control line at the tack of the mainsail used to tighten the luff. See "downhaul."

**cunningham hole**          Heavy grommet sewn in the luff at foot of sail to absorb the load. The sail can be pulled down with lanyards to adjust the sail draft.

**curl**          Too much curve: in a spinnaker's luff or leech, in a mainsail leech or in the jib foot.

**cutter**          Single-masted vessel with two headsails.

**davit**          Small crane used to hoist a dinghy or anchor aboard; hangs out over side or stern.

**dead reckoning (DR)**          Method used to determine where you are, without using navigational tools. Employs the records of course sailed, distance run and time spanned, among other things. And don't forget the charts. A "must learn" topic for every crew member.

**depth sounder**          See "fathometer."

**DF radio (RDF)**          Radio fitted with a direction finder antenna. Great for shore sailing (with the chart in hand, of course).

| | |
|---|---|
| **displacement** | 1) The weight of the water displaced by the floating hull, equal to the actual weight of the hull; |
| | 2) A close estimate of the vessel's weight. |
| **dodger** | Canvas "sun room" which gives overhead protection for the hatchway and part of the cockpit. Worth its weight in gold during messy weather! |
| **dog (a hatch)** | Mechanical device to secure hatch; "to dog" is to firmly secure. **Do this** in high seas! |
| **doghouse** | Instead of a dodger, this structure, usually with windows, is permanently built over companionway or cockpit. |
| **dorade box** | A box built over a hole in the hull which allows air (but not water) to enter the cabin. Has built-in baffles and pre-cut drain holes. Used as ventilator. |
| **douse (to)** | Lower or slacken sail suddenly. |
| **downhaul** | 1) Line used for pulling down a sail; |
| | 2) Fitting or control line at the tack of the mainsail to tighten the luff; |
| | 3) Control line to pull down the main boom on its goose-neck slide. |
| **draft** | 1) Depth of water needed to float the boat; |
| | 2) The amount of curve in a sail. |
| **drag (to)** | When the anchor fails to hold the boat in place. A real drag when it happens. |
| **drag** | Resistance caused by the forward motion of the boat through the water. |

| | |
|---|---|
| **drifter** | Ultra-lightweight headsail sometimes used instead of a spinnaker or genoa. |
| **echo sounder** | See "fathometer." |
| **EPIRB** | Emergency Position Indicating Radio Beacon. If you have no other survival equipment on board, have an EPIRB. There are many levels to consider; get the best you can afford. At time of publication, the 406 MHz is considered state-of-the-art. |
| **ensign** | Nationality flag flown by a vessel. |
| **eye** | 1) A closed loop;<br><br>2) The direction from which the wind is blowing. |
| **eye bolt** | Sturdy bolt with a ring at the end. |
| **fall off (to)** | Put the helm up (windward); turn the bow of the boat away from the wind. Also see "sail off." |
| **fathom** | The measure of water depth: 1 fathom = 6 feet. |
| **fathometer** | Terminology is the principal concept here. You probably know it as either "sonar" or "depth sounder." Also called an echo sounder. Electronic device which determines water depth by measuring the time taken by a sound signal to go to the seabed and back again. "Fathometer" is actually a trade name, but used more in the U.S.A. than "echo sounder." |
| **fender** | Cushion used to protect the hull when coming into dock or tying alongside another vessel. Usually plastic, cork or hemp. |
| **fid** | A tool used to separate the strands of a synthetic line and help weave a loop on the line. |

| | |
|---|---|
| **fiddle** | The lip around the edge of a table or surface to keep things from sliding off. Have it at least 1" high. |
| **fluke** | Pointed ends of the anchor arms which bite into the ground. |
| **fo'c'sle** | Means "forecastle." Area forward of the mast. |
| **foot** | The bottom edge of a sail from tack to clew. |
| **foreguy** | Line used as a downhaul on spinnaker pole. |
| **forestay** | See "headstay." |
| **foretriangle** | The triangle area formed by the mast, the headstay and the deck. |
| **freeboard** | The height of a vessel's exposed hull above water. |
| **furl (to)** | To fold up/roll up and stop a sail. See "stop." |
| **gallows** | Permanent framework for the end of the boom to rest on when the mainsail is lowered. |
| **genoa** | Large triangular headsail, 150% or larger. By itself it can fill the foretriangle or more; extends well aft of the shrouds. As the largest headsail, it's a biggee and a bear to handle alone. (Also see "sail/percent ratio.") |
| **ghosting** | Making way in super light air. |
| **gimbal** | Using pins, rings and pivots, this is a device to keep level the compass, lamps, table, etc., no matter how yucky the seas. |
| **gimbal stove** | The above, applied to the stove. A must. Keep on hand two pot brackets or clamps per burner. |
| **gooseneck** | The universal joint which holds the boom to the mast. Don't EVER leave home without it. |

| | |
|---|---|
| **grinder** | Large high-powered pedestal winch; also, the crewman who operates it. Both mostly found on hi-tech racing vessels. |
| **grommet** | A metal eye in a sail used to attach sheets, tack and clew pins, reef points, etc. |
| **gunwale** | The upper <u>edge</u> of the side of the hull where the hull and the deck meet. |
| **guy** | A line that straddles the spinnaker pole and holds it in a horizontal position. "Guy" is a term addressed to lines for spinnaker sails. See "afterguy," "lazy guy." |
| **gybe (to)** | See "jibe." |
| **gypsy** | Wheel on a windlass with recesses to hold links of a chain (mostly found on anchor winches). See "windlass." |
| **halyard** | Wire or line used for hoisting a sail or flag. Not to be confused with "lanyard." |
| **hanks** | Clip used to hold the luff of a sail to a stay. The sail which is held to the stay with hanks is referred to as "hanked on." Logical! |
| **hard up, hard down** | The position of the helm (tiller or wheel); as far as possible to windward or leeward, respectively. |
| **head** | The other meaning: The top of the sail. |
| **headstay** | A wire mast support running from the masthead to the bow, to keep the mast from falling aft. |
| **heave to** | To trim sails and helm so vessel lies as stationary as possible. |
| **heel (to)** | To incline from the perpendicular (the vessel, preferably!) |

**hoist**                    Vertical edge or measurement of sail.

**hoist (to)**               Haul it up!

**holiday**                  The spot(s) you missed when you painted or varnished.

**holystone**                Block of sandstone used for scrubbing the deck. The Captain does this the best.

**irons (in)**               Stopped dead in its tracks, the vessel will not respond on any tack. Head is to the wind.

**iron wind**                Cutesy name meaning "Sailboat under motor power."

**jam cleat**                Self-securing *friction* holding device for lines. See "cam cleat."

**jib**                      The foremost headsail.

                             *TIP: When winding the jib sheets on cockpit winches, they always go clockwise, port and starboard.*

**jibe (to)**                Just the opposite of tacking and what you normally don't want to do. Bringing the **STERN** into the eye of the wind, rather than the bow, and the boom lunges across…fast.

                             *Of course, sometimes jibing is necessary, as when, if you don't you'll run aground. In that case, go for it…but be controlled and PAY ATTENTION!*

**jury-rig (to)**            To erect, construct and arrange in a makeshift fashion. That's what the dictionary says. What that means is to make do with what you have on board.

**kedge**                    See "lunch hook."

**ketch**            Loosely speaking, a two-masted vessel, fore-and-aft rigged, with mizzenmast stepped forward of the rudderpost.

Not so loosely, the mizzenmast is stepped forward of the after end of the waterline and is shorter than the mainmast.

**knot**             Measurement of speed at sea: A knot equals one nautical mile which is approx. 6080 ft. per hour.

**laminate**         Material built up in layers such as fiberglass or plywood. You do NOT want to find "de-lamination!"

**lanyard**          A short line used to set up a shroud or some other part of the rigging. Used to extend shrouds or stays.

**lapstrake**        Type of hull construction where skin planks overlap one another.

**latitude**         The distance north or south of the equator expressed in degrees. See your Nav teacher for further details.

**lazy guy**         No, not the goof-off on board. This is the secondary line attached to the tack and clew of the spinnaker. Used to free the primary line during jibing.

Okay, okay, so it's the goof-off on board—Cheesh!!

**lead**             Pronounced "leed." A block or eye controlling direction of sail trim.

**lead**             Pronounced "led." A weight on a marked line used for taking soundings. See "cast (to)."

**leading edge**     Foremost edge of a sail.

**leeboard**         See "bunkboard."

**leech**            The aftermost part of a sail which is the trailing edge.

**leeward**          The opposite direction from which the wind is coming.

**leeway**           Sliding to leeward, you are going perpendicular to the course you are trying to steer.  Also called "crabbing" for obvious reasons, if you've ever seen a crab underway.

**lifeline**         1) A line through stanchions along the sides of the deck used to prevent unplanned "man overboard!" drills;

2) Line secured to the crew person as added safety precautions during heavy sailing. When at sea and when on deck, **ALWAYS WEAR AND SECURE IT**!

*We have a rule on "Whither Thou": The life line gets unhooked only when the wearer is midway **down** the ladder; it gets hooked to the lifeline ring mounted on the cockpit sole when the wearer is midway **out**. Not a bad rule to adopt for your own vessel.*

**lift**             1) Vertical control line; used for both spinnaker pole and end of main boom. See "topping lift";

2) Change in wind direction which allows the vessel to point higher, or to ease the sail trim without changing course. Neat when it happens!

**LOA**              Length overall: extreme length of the hull.

**longitude**        Distance east/west of Greenwich meridian expressed in degrees. Go see your Nav teacher, etc.

**luff**             The forward part of a sail between the head and the tack.

**luff tension**     Pressure exerted on the luff to adjust draft location.

**luff (to)**        To put the helm down and bring the bow closest to (or actually into) the wind.

**luffing**          The flapping of sails when not trimmed properly. A no-no.

**lunch hook**
Sometimes called a kedge, this is a small anchor usually fitted with a line instead of a chain, and not intended for heavy-duty or long-time mooring. Also can be used to haul a vessel off when she has gone aground.

**LWL**
Load water line. The length of the hull where it sits loaded in the water. Also the line where the designer <u>meant</u> it to sit loaded in the water. Rather nice when both are in the same place!

**marlinspike**
Pointed instrument used to separate a 3-braided line; also for tightening or loosening shackle pins. You will no doubt become very familiar with this goodie (along with a fid).

**meridian**
A true north/south line. Nav person!...

**mid-boom traveler**
Sliding device located beneath boom at its mid-point, attached to it by the mainsheet. Controls the athwartships position of the sail.

**mizzen**
Sail similar to the main in shape but smaller. Mounted on its own mast and boom-rigged near the stern of a ketch or yawl.

**off the wind**
Not close hauled.

**on the wind**
Close hauled.

**one-off**
Shortcut lingo meaning a "one of a kind" custom-design boat.

**outhaul**
A device used for pulling the clew of the mainsail out on the boom.

**painter**
The line on the dinghy bow used to secure it.

**paraffin**
Diesel kerosene. A British term, old chap.

**pay out(to)**
To ease away; to slack out.

**pelican hook**          A jointed hook with a pivot pin held closed by a ring.
      Knocking the ring back releases the hold even under great
                          strain. Usually used on mizzen backstays and gangway
                          lifelines.

**pinch (to)**            Sailing too close to the wind. Ease off!

**pitchpole**             Capsizing the vessel 360° ***end over end***. No way to start
                          your day and could end it fast. Not too great on the mast
                          and rigging either.

**point (to)**            Getting as close to the wind as possible.  See "close
                          hauled."

**poop (to)**             An overtaking sea which has crested, then breaks over the
                          stern and momentarily buries the boat. WET!

**port tack**             No, not *heeling* to port. Port tack is when the boom is to
                          starboard and *the wind* is coming over the port side.

**preventer**             Any line, chain, or fitting which backs up and limits the
                          movement of whatever you want to limit (rigging, spars,
                          cables, etc.).

**pulpit**                A structure of tubing on the bow or bowsprit; gives a
                          reasonably secured (pseudo-fenced) place to work while
                          changing headsails.

**range marks**           Practice this for going in and out of harbors. Also helps in
                          becoming familiar with the compass.

**RDF  radio**            See DF Radio.

**reach**                 The wind is abeam or forward of the beam, but not forward
                          enough to be close hauled.

| | |
|---|---|
| **reacher** | Can be either a flat spinnaker or a lightweight high-clewed headsail used to reach. |
| **reef** | Reduce the area of a sail by tying or rolling down a part of it. Also called "to shorten sail." |
| **reef points** | Short lines attached to the mainsail used to tie in a reef. |
| **reeve (to)** | Passing a line through a block or hole of any kind. |
| **rhumb line** | The shortest distance between two sailing points. |
| **roach** | The outward curve sometimes found in the leech of a sail. Battens in the sail hold the shape. |
| **rode (anchor)** | The chain or line (cable) which attaches the anchor to the vessel. |
| **roller furling** | Mechanical system which rolls the jib around its own luff wire. Fine in controlled waters but can be a problem at sea. Out there, the pressure exerted by strong winds on the rolled up jib can literally break the headstay. |
| **roller reefing** | Another mechanical system: this one reduces the mainsail by rolling the sail around the boom. But…as above, the more mechanics aboard, the more to go wrong, right? |
| | Re-consider these for bluewater sailing, gang. |
| **rounding up** | Action of the vessel as it turns toward the wind. Usually means a BIG angle of change. This is *not* fun. |
| **rubber-banding** | A method to "stop" or control sails; usually associated with spinnakers but can also be used with a large mainsail such as a genoa. See "stop." |
| **run before (to)** | Run dead downwind before a gale or hard squall. |
| **run (to)** | To sail before the wind. |

| | |
|---|---|
| **sail off (to)** | To turn away from the wind. See "fall off (to)." |
| **sail (percent/ratio)** | When sail is described as, for example, 65-75% (see "storm jib") or 150% (see "genoa"), those percentages are based on the 100% area of the foretriangle. |
| **schooner** | Two-masted vessel with the mainmast as tall or taller than the foremast. |
| **scope** | The length of line or chain by which the boat is anchored. |
| **scull (to)** | Method to propel a boat by working an oar from side to side, or doing the same with the rudder. *Verboten* in a race. |
| **scupper(s)** | Holes in the toe rail which allow water to drain from the deck. |
| **sea** | A wave, as in a "following sea." Means the waves are going in the same direction you are. Fast, furious and wild! |
| **sea anchor** | 1) A comical conical canvas bag let out behind the vessel meant to help slow it down. Sometimes works, sometimes doesn't, **always** impossible to pull back aboard while running! |
| | 2) Any device (rode, tires, etc.) that keeps the boat running with the waves but tries to slow it down at the same time. |
| **sea cock** | A valve meant to prevent sea water from entering a through-hull fitting. |
| **shackle** | A metal U-shaped fitting with an eye in each of its arms through which you drive or screw a pin. |
| **shake out (to)** | Let out a reef. |
| **shank** | The part of the anchor which joins the arms to the ring. In other words, the anchor shaft. |

| | |
|---|---|
| **shear pin** | One of a boat's "sacrificial lambs." In this case it is an easily replaceable pin meant to break under stress; used to protect the propeller of an outboard motor. |
| **sheave** | The pulley wheel for turning a sheet or halyard. |
| **sheer** | The curve of the gunwale. |
| **sheet** | The line controlling the trim of a sail. |
| **sheet lead** | Pronounced "leed." A device, such as a block, controlling the angle and direction of the sheet to the sail to help shape it. |
| **shifting backstay** | Pretty much what the name implies: A backstay that can be changed to tighten or ease the tension according to wind direction. |
| **shorten sail** | See "reef." |
| **shroud(s)** | The athwartship supports of the mast. With the aid of the vital chain plates, prevents the mast from falling sideways. |
| **side light(s)** | Your running lights. |
| **sight** | Observation done by sextant or compass to obtain a position line. Nav teacher! |
| **slack** | To ease or pay out a line. |
| **sloop** | A single-masted vessel with one headstay. |
| **snatch block** | A block that is hinged at the neck so it can easily be opened for line insertion. |
| **snub (to)** | Check. Line. Slowly. |
| **snugged down** | Well-reefed under a small (but comfy) sail area. |

| | |
|---|---|
| **sounding** | 1) Measuring the depth of water;<br><br>2) The resulting figure as marked on a chart. |
| **spreaders** | Wooden or metal struts on the mast to give the shrouds more mechanical advantage to support the mast. |
| **spring line** | The dock lines used to keep the boat secured and minimize forward/backward motion. Incorporate, please, as part of your own good neighbor policy. |
| **stanchion** | Metal lifeline supports mounted on deck or bulwarks. |
| **starboard tack** | See "port tack" and lean the other way. |
| **stay** | A part of the standing rigging that supports the mast fore and aft. See "headstay" and "backstay." |
| **step** | 1) The part that holds the base of the mast to the deck;<br><br>2) "To step": to install the mast;<br><br>3) Step(mast): a way to get up to the top of the mast. |
| **stiff** | Term describing a boat that resists heeling forces; a boat that likes to stand up straight. Opposite of "tender (1)." |
| **stop** | A weak binding designed to break easily which is put around a spinnaker, to be hoisted now but unfurled later. When the sail is needed, the "ForeDeckus Apeus Americus" need only give a good pull to break the stops. |
| **storm jib** | The smallest jib (usually 65-75%) used in the absolutely, without a doubt, unequivocally lousiest weather. |
| **stringer** | Material running longitudinally from bow to stern to stiffen the hull and prevent bowing ("bowing": as in banana-shaped). |

| | |
|---|---|
| **strut** | A structural piece designed to resist pressure in the direction of its length. |
| **swell** | Long easy waves with no breaking crests. A swell way to sail! |
| **tabernacle** | Housing located on the deck for the heel and pivot to permit lowering the mast. If you go under a lot of bridges, this is the only way. |
| **tack** | You know this as a point of sailing. It also means the lower forward corner of a fore-and-aft sail. |
| **tackle** | As in "block and…." Consists of two blocks with line reeved through each; used as a mechanical advantage. I love mechanical advantages! |
| **take up (to)** | To make taut. |
| **tang** | Fitting (usually metal) on mast or hull to which the rigging is attached. |
| **tender** | 1) A boat which heels excessively, even in average winds. Touchy… |
| | 2) A term given to the vessel-to-shore-and-back-again craft. |
| **thimble** | Grooved metal or plastic shape used inside an eye splice to prevent chafing. |
| **topping lift** | The line or wire used to support the out-board end of the boom while sail is being set or doused; also takes the weight of the boom in a seaway. |
| **transom** | Athwartships section at the stern. In other words, de tush of de vessel. |

| | |
|---|---|
| **trim** | Adjusting sail relative to the vessel's centerline; to take in on the jibsheet or mainsheet. |
| **trough** | The valley between two seas. Can be D-E-E-P. |
| **turnbuckle** | Adjustable screw device to control tension on stays, shrouds and other rigging. |
| **turning block** | 1) The block located on the quarter or transom that leads a sheet or guy forward to a winch; <br><br> 2) Any block on deck that allows a bend in a line. |
| **turtle** | The bag that holds the spinnaker. Pack it right every time, please. |
| **turtle (to turn)** | Capsizing the boat 360° *side to side*. This DOES ruin your whole day! |
| **under bare poles** | Under way without any sails set, running with the wind, but without the "Iron Wind." Can be White Knuckle Time. |
| **vang (boom)** | A device meant to pull down the main boom and tighten the leech when the mainsheet cannot do it by itself. |
| **variation** | The difference between true and magnetic north at a given place. Uh, Nav person…. |
| **warp** | Strong line attached to an anchor or dock. |
| **washboards** | A term given to louvered hatchcovers on the companionway that resemble the old-fashioned "washboard" Great-GrandMama used to use. |
| **weather helm** | A vessel with a tendency to turn her bow into the wind is said to have "weather helm." Hard helm work at times. |
| **weather (to)** | Approaching close hauled. Also referred to as "going to weather." |

| | |
|---|---|
| **weatherly** | Describes a vessel capable of sailing close to the wind. A good feature. |
| **whisker pole** | A strut used to keep either the spinnaker or large genoa clew under control while running downwind. |
| **windlass** | A winch with a horizontal drum, fitted with a gypsy for handling the anchor's chain cable. |
| **wing-on-wing** | Two headsails, one to starboard, one to port, for downwind configuration (can be used in lieu of a spinnaker). |
| **working sails** | The sails used when cruising (as opposed to racing or ultra-light sails). |

*TIP: Tanbark (a maroon red) is easier to see at night (surprisingly!), and is also easier on the eyes during midday when the sun is at its most merciless.*

| | |
|---|---|
| **yankee jib** | A large high-cut triangular headsail meant for light or moderate winds. |
| **yaw (to)** | To wobble about on either side of the intended course. *Tackeee.* |
| **yawl** | Two masted vessel; mizzenmast is aft of the rudder and is shorter than the main mast. |
| **zinc** | Another "sacrificial lamb." When various metals, which are in contact with each other, come into contact with salt water, they can develop into a DC battery. When this occurs, the weakest metal involved is destroyed. Zinc, being weaker than bronze, is attached to the propeller shaft. These zincs are relatively inexpensive and easily replaceable. Do so as often as needed to save that expensive bronze prop and shaft! However, don't think that if two zincs are good, twelve will be better. Too many and you negate the polarity effect and reverse the result. |

There, that wasn't so bad! As I said, shallow wading. This is by no means a complete lingo review, but you will pick up detailed navigational terms and the not-so-frequently heard terms as you go along. By becoming familiar and comfortable with the above, though, you will find life at sea to be less hassle and much more genial and meaningful.

## TIPS TO LESSEN CONFUSION

| *If you remember that:* | *It's easy to determine:* |
| --- | --- |
| The words *left* and *port* both have four letters | "Port" vs. "Starboard" |
| *Red* is *port;* both are the shortest words | Red vs. Green running lights |

There is a saying: "RED  RIGHT *RETURNING*": Therefore, going **OUT,** the red is on the **LEFT.**  Right?  Correct.

*Tanbark Working Sails*

### THE MARINE (PHONETIC) SPELLING ALPHABET
### USED IN ALL COMMUNICATIONS AND TRANSMISSIONS

| | |
|---|---|
| ALPHA | NOVEMBER |
| BRAVO | OSCAR |
| CHARLIE | PAPA |
| DELTA | QUEBEC |
| ECHO | ROMEO |
| FOX | SIERRA |
| GOLF | TANGO |
| HOTEL | UNIFORM |
| INDIA | VICTOR |
| JULIETTE | WHISKEY |
| KILO | X-RAY |
| LIMA | YANKEE |
| MIKE | ZULU |

### *GETTING YOUR FEET WET Continues*

Almost there. But before we leave this preliminary portion, here is a light touch on a few of your responsibilities for those times when you are…

### *OUT OF THE GALLEY*

You will be assisting the Captain standing watch, lending a second pair of hands at repair time, mending sails if need be, helping to hoist the Skipper to the top of the mast for minor repairs (or, if you're light enough, he hoists you). As First Mate, you will not only support his plans and the methods to those plans, but you will be capable of making independent decisions in the event of an emergency.

It is vital to learn the potential trouble spots and know where all spare parts are kept. What does each part represent? Discuss with the Skipper: When there are no actual spare parts, how *do* you do simple repairs, using your combined ingenuity to make do with equipment and material on board?

Know your boat, Mate, from bowsprit to transom. Oh, I agree: All that deck paraphernalia, unfamiliar hardware and an instrument panel that rivals the Concorde can be a bit overwhelming. But so is a well-equipped kitchen to a novice cook, remember? You managed to come to terms then; you will here, too.

For starters, find all the signalling gear: horns, bells, spotlights. Learn the correct way to operate the VHF radio, both for emergencies and on a daily basis. Then, once those items are understood, continue with the rest of the technical apparatus aboard. Your efficiency and sense of self-worth will skyrocket if you acquire an elementary knowledge of the following:

- All deck fittings and boat hardware

- Engine or auxiliary power

- Electrical and mechanical systems

- Water pumps and system (usually super simple)

- The stove, of course

- **ALL** radio and electronic equipment

- The head

- Outboard motor for dinghy: operating it and making simple repairs

- The belowdecks ins-and-outs of both the electrical panel and the battery set-ups

- Sea valve locations and their operation (open/close)

Keep permanent notes as each part and apparatus becomes more familiar. Read the manuals that come with the gear, and *always ask questions*: of the Skipper, and of your experienced boating friends as well. Ask the manufacturer for clarification of terminology you do not understand, but be aware…they do not always give the most impartial advice.

When running a smoothly functioning home, we know familiar sounds and hums that tell us all is well; likewise, we are quick to hear the hiccup telling us there is potential trouble brewing. It's the same on a boat; we can often be the ones who first hear (or smell) something out of whack. When this happens, more knowledge of gear and equipment equates to a more efficient solution to a potential problem, using four hands instead of two.

More importantly, all of us fret over what would occur should something happen to the Skipper and we are the one suddenly in charge. This is a normal worry and shared by all First Mates. This worry **will** diminish, or at least greatly decrease as your knowledge, experience and confidence grows. Trust me.

In the next chapter, there is an overview list of supplies to consider having on board for emergency repairs. If you do not understand any of these, read up on them. And the list is by no means complete; you will no doubt think of many other items. (We had a dear friend of ours, prior to Gene's singlehanded race, ask where we kept the spare mast!)

Okay! So much for the preliminaries. Time to take a look at the boat and the crew as a whole.

*"If we let things terrify us, life will not be worth living."*                              *— Seneca*

# 3

*YOU AND YOUR BOAT AS A WHOLE or*
*SKIPPER, THIS ONE'S FOR YOU!*

*Getting Ready for Bluewater*

*The Vessel In General*

*Now A Detailed Look:*
*Radio Aids—Spare Parts—Repair Kits—Tools—Emergency Gear*

*You and Your Crew*

*"There is nothing—absolutely nothing—half so much worth doing as simply messing about in boats."*
*— Kenneth Grahame*

## *GETTING READY FOR BLUEWATER*

You can't be too prepared. This is not only an undeniable statement when readying for serious sailing, but was also the title of Gene's article, published in *Cruising World* a bit back. His tips and suggestions are just as timely now, and the information and suggestions given then are broad enough to apply to any offshore cruising team or crew.

This is why most of what follows in this chapter is directed to the Skipper. Please, First Mate, share these pages with him. It will make your job that much easier, and just might give him additional ideas and/or concepts, as well as add to his general food for thought.

None of what follows is cast in stone, of course, but rather a broad spectrum being offered for *your* consideration with reference to *you*, *your* crew, and *your* vessel.

Enter, Gene:

## *YOUR VESSEL IN GENERAL*

Let's begin with your boat. Unless you are so wealthy that you can afford to design and build a boat from scratch, you had better take a long hard look at your present vessel…the same faithful friend in which you've bobbed the bay or lake on warm, sunny Sundays.

"There is a formidable spectrum of boats in the water these days, from those designed to sail to, and in, any waters anywhere in the world, de-escalating to those docile vessels that have no business being out in anything more than a 5-knot wind on a mirrored pond. The unfortunate dilemma is that even those manufacturers sometimes tout their product as "*SEAWORTHY BY GOD SHE'LL DO GREAT OUT THERE , MAN—NO PROBLEM!*"

Sure.

"Face it: No boat is perfect. But to adapt a vessel mainly used until now for gentle day sailing, to ready that vessel for bluewater serious sailing, steps need to be taken at the beginning. Questions need to be asked and then answered honestly, questions such as:

- How many owners has this vessel had?

- *Where* has she sailed and in *what kinds* of waters and weather?

- How many actual sailing hours does she have on her existing rigging?

- What is the present condition of her hull, her deck and her bulkheads?

"Chances are, you will be pleased with your answers, but ask and answer the questions **now**, so time is on your side, to make sure there is enough, without undue pressure, to fortify and follow through on your findings. Your life, the life of your crew and the vessel itself may depend on your honest evaluation.

"With your answers and subsequent evaluations, and always remembering your vessel *must be bluewater seaworthy*, consider these absolute facts:

Aged parts can fail at a faster rate at sea;
The least expected problem WILL happen (Murphy's Law);
Your critique is probably overrated."

*"A good exterior is a silent recommendation."*                    — *P. Syrus*

### NOW A DETAILED LOOK

Time to do some hardheaded review. Get a notebook, put on your grubbies and get out the bosun's chair.

"If the backstays need to be beefed up, replace them: do not assume your present set will do (unless they are brand new). If at all worn and/or ready for replacement, do so. Also consider the next larger size.

"Check every turnbuckle, every single square inch of mast and spreaders. Either plan an underwater trip yourself, hire a diver to do the same minute scrutiny on the hull and keel while in the water, or plan a major boat outhaul. In either case, a total in-depth review from keel to masthead should be a major part of your plans.

"Go over each sail with a sharp eye for the slightest weakness, fray or needed reinforcement. Schedule any repairs or replacements with your favorite sailmaker *now*. Talk to them, explain your plans. They are experts and can give invaluable advice, with skills to create what *you* need in canvas.

"Look for the not-so-obvious fault as well as those that stare at you day after day; 'obvious' meaning the visible jibsheet beginning to fray, that noisy halyard winch groaning for a lube job. But what about your out-of-sight water tank? Is it housed so it positively *will not* come loose?"

[Dottie: Gene is hyper on water tanks. In his first TransPac race a loosened water tank was beating his 26' "Pretz" to death inside the port bow, as the violent action of the Pacific shelf waters pounded the exterior hull. A miraculous watchful guardian angel sat on his shoulder that day that helped him to make the awful but vital soul-wrenching decision: turn back. "Pretz" might not have lasted another day; with a ruptured tank losing precious water, more than a dream would have been lost.]

"What about the grommets and hanks on each sail? What about the masthead tang? What about each inch of spars and rigging? Travel up and down your mast, <u>slowly</u> <u>and</u> <u>many</u> <u>times</u>, checking everything in every direction.

"Is the cockpit set up to be self-draining? It better be, out there. This **cannot be over-emphasized!** Does the vessel have complete watertight integrity through-hull fittings which are properly installed, with easily workable valves? (Plug-type seacock valves are preferable). Are all hoses attached with two—yes, two—stainless steel hose clamps whenever possible? Are all pieces of heavy gear (anchors, batteries, fuel tanks) secured so it **positively cannot shift or come loose**, no matter how severe the seas?

"Has all wiring been minutely inspected? Electrical components are among the first things to go awry during heavy weather.

"A most important electrical consideration is a solar panel. This is one modern device no bluewater vessel should be without. It can recharge a battery when the motor cannot start without battery assistance, and it can operate a VHF or a SatNav system during daylight hours. Here, sound investigation and good questions on your part will give you confidence in the system you choose to mount in your vessel.

"Which system? Talk to your sailing friends, read your local sailing "bible" such as *Latitude 38* published in Sausalito, California, and considered by Northern California sailors as the best sailing information available, mentioned here as the most familiar to the skipper and crew of "Whither Thou." Suggest you do not ask the various manufacturers…they are not known to give unbiased information.

"Can you climb the mast easily if necessary? Consider a rope step system, permanent mast steps, or at the very least a hoisted ladder or bosun's chair with the proper tackle to use it.

"Take a page out of the west coast singlehander's book when he is preparing for the TransPac: In order to qualify, as either a first-time racer or a seasoned racer in a different vessel, he must complete a 400-mile solo. You need not solo, in fact it is best if the planned seagoing crew does this together, but between now and your departure date, make this run as often as you can. Shake that vessel down, hard.

"Put all parts through as demanding a test as you can devise, as many times as possible."

> [Dottie: Although contrary to Gene's above statement directed to the Skipper of the vessel, I strongly recommend that you to do at least one extensive solo stint, "extensive" meaning a minimum of 24 hours out of sheltered and familiar waters, "solo" meaning *you*, babe.
>
> Don't panic. "Solo" need not mean being out there all night all by your lonesome. In this case, "solo" means being in complete charge. Your Skipper can be aboard, but he is to be a passenger only. Agree beforehand that YOU are in charge of every decision and action, and he is to stay out of it. But for safety's sake and to help your peace of mind, he is there if needed. Remember though: no help or advice from him until you **ask for** and **want** that help or advice!
>
> This will help bolster your own confidence and ability, so important because, as we talked about back in "Out of the Galley," there could conceivably come a time when you are the one that has to get that vessel back to shore safely, should the Captain be unable to. Please give this suggestion serious consideration.]

"You don't have to go out in a raging hurricane or ignore the Coast Guard warning when they advise you to stay put, but when the weather is less than perfect, get out your foul weather gear and go sailing. I'll say it again: Merely sailing in smooth waters on a warm, sunny Sunday won't show you a thing."

## RADIO AIDS

> [Dottie: A VHF radio is considered a must, even though the scope and range of communication is limited. It will transmit and receive emergency messages on Channel 16 up to 100 miles (maybe more, depending on the height of the mast and/or the weather). Familiar-

ize yourselves with all the channels and which ones are used for
what: ship-to-ship, ship-to-shore, Coast Guard transmissions only,
shipping traffic, etc.]

Gene again:

"Perhaps you have sophisticated navigation gear aboard, such as a SatNav or a
Loran. Super. Although SatNavs operate efficiently on a worldwide satellite system,
Lorans are more restricted. Both, however, involve electronics that have been known
to fail. Basic sextant knowledge, an accurate and reliable timepiece set at Greenwich
Mean Time, and dead reckoning skills have stood many a sailor in good stead long
before the advance of modern technology. Do yourself a favor: Learn the working end
of basic navigation for human (mechanical) override, should the need arise, and keep
a 24-hour dead reckoning log.

"Again: Check with your local Coast Guard unit or local college and find out
what navigation classes they offer. It is worth it for you, Skipper, _and_ all members
of your crew."

### SPARE PARTS

[Dottie: Do not limit yourself to minimums; have spare parts kits
on board for just about everything, including: sewing and sail repair,
electrical repair, plumbing, hull repair, engine repair with separate
engine tools, stove repair, bilge pump parts, self-steering vane
replacements…to name just a few.]

(Spare mast, anyone? Oh COME ON!)

Gene:

"Think about spares and apply the "what ifs": 'What if I didn't have a particular spare part, could I jury-rig one and continue on, using good sailing horse sense?  If something breaks or fails, and I can't fix it, can I continue without it?' Only experience can answer this for each of us. Here you must review your total system, for only *you* can decide what to carry. To that end then, here is some food for thought and consideration for additional or spare equipment:

- HEAVY WEATHER SAILS

- FITTINGS OF EVERY KIND, especially winch handles, blocks, shackles, pins, turnbuckles, chains and toggles

- LINES, SHEETS, RODES AND WARPS

- EMERGENCY TILLER

- STEERING CABLE

- AUXILIARY STEERING

- STAY OR SHROUD REPLACEMENT

- MISCELLANEOUS HARDWARE AND FASTENINGS OF EVERY KIND

- ANCHORS,  INCLUDING A SEA ANCHOR

- SAIL STOPS, SHOCK CORD AND SHORT LINES

- TACKLES, VANG GEAR, PREVENTERS AND CHAFE GUARDS

- HORN, FLASHLIGHT(S), ALL  WITH EXTRA BATTERIES

- RADIO AND SIGNAL GEAR

- PUMPS, BUCKETS AND BAILER

## *REPAIR KITS*

- **sewing and sail**

  thread, twine, marlinspike, needles, fiddle, palm, tapes, patches, beeswax, sail slides, hanks, sail shackles, scraps of leather

- **electrical**

  bulbs, fuses, electrical tape, copper wire, batteries, circuit tester, solder and solder iron (NOT electric), radio parts

- **plumbing**

  hose clamps, spare head parts and all pump parts, syphon hose, packing grease (and wooden plugs for sure).

- **hull repair**

  caulking cotton, bedding and seam compound, foam rubber, plywood sheets, regular putty, cup grease, soft metal sheets, plastic steel, self-curing urethane putty, fiberglass tape and resin, canvas, epoxy adhesive

- **engine/gasoline**

  points, condenser, rotor, water pump, seal, impeller, distributor cap, coil, spark plugs, belts

- **engine/diesel**

  injectors, starting motor system, fuel filters, fuel pump, injector feed lines

- **engine tools**

    gauges, spanners and crank handle, lube oil

- **miscellaneous**

    stove parts

    patch kit for the raft or dinghy

    extra parts for self steering vane

"I suggest as a reference that you review the equipment requirements for the various TransPacific races. If the racers do not have these items, they are not allowed to race. This will give you a broad idea of what the pros regard as basic.

## *TOOLS, GENERAL*

Assorted sizes of screw drivers, wrenches, pliers and hammer; wood saw, hack saw with spare blades, wire cutter, bolt cutter, wrecking bar, hatchet, brace and bits, drill and bits, tin snips, chisels, files, plane, clamps, vise, crimping tool for compressing sleeves on wire cables.

("**Pliers** might also include large C-type w/adjustable jaws, needle-nose, vise grip. **Wrenches** might also include monkey, Stillson, end, socket, spark plug and chain wrench.

*TIP: The end wrench must be large enough to fit the largest nut on the boat. Try it out now to make sure it fits."*)

### *EMERGENCY GEAR*

- EPIRB (a must)

- FIRE EXTINGUISHERS

- LIFE JACKETS AND LIFE HARNESS

- EMERGENCY WATER PUMPS

- THE LIFE SYSTEM already discussed

- FLARES, both the kind shot from a pistol and the hand-held type, although the latter are much less effective: too close to the deck/ surface of the water for good visibility. Still, they are better than nothing.

- ADDITIONAL VISUAL DISTRESS SIGNALS: e.g.,

  Flashing strobe light mounted to the top of the mast

  Spotlight (in addition to normal supply of flashlights)

  Orange smoke signals for daytime use

  Personal strobes, either worn around the neck or fastened to your person in some fashion

- A WET SUIT

- STAPLING GUN (heavy duty) with stainless steel staples <u>OR</u> self-tapping screws

- SHEETS OF LIGHTWEIGHT PLYWOOD

- SHEETS OF COPPER AND LEAD

- POLES OR EXTRA SPARS (spinnaker pole)

- CAULKING COMPOUND for use under water

- STRONG TOPPING LIFT, controllable from the deck

- EXTRA CHAIN, suitable for emergency repairs

- EXTRA SUPPLY OF BATTERIES for everything

"Above all, Skipper, you and all those on board should know where all the stowage is. Make sure there is immediate and clear access to the storage area."

*"Things are only worth what you make them worth."*                                        *— Moliere*

### *YOU AND YOUR CREW*

Again, Gene:

Okay, Skipper, now it's your turn. Age means very little; it is the physical and mental critique which is crucial. Remember: You and your crew, following your directions, are the only ones who can think and make decisions: decisions about weather, sail changes, boat speed, navigational maneuvers through coastal tanker lanes and currents, and overall navigation using your sextant, chronometer, VHF and whatever other navigational aids you have. The vessel doesn't do the deciding; you do. She can only do what you ask her to do.

"Be at your peak physical level, or admit the physical level you are at. Your fitness will be repeatedly tested as you and the vessel work together. As with most other things in life, good health and prime condition is a ladder, **with you and your doctor knowing which is your individual rung.** It isn't necessary to be the world's greatest athlete to be an offshore sailor, but **respect your own limitations and sail to them.**

"I had the privilege of sailing and sharing a quaff or two with a singlehander who did three races; my two and one other. These were done *after* a total of two—count them—two open heart surgeries. He wouldn't make an Olympic team, but he sure as hell raced and sailed with the best...and did *his* best. Got his private pilot license reinstalled, as well. Cheers to you, Harold U of Joshua H."

*"Use your health, even to the point of wearing it out. That is what it is for. Spend all you have before you die; and do not outlive yourself."*                      — George Bernard Shaw

"How you get and keep in shape is up to you. Continue or increase your normal activity program: Walk, jog, swim, hike, go to the gym, lift weights. You decide, **but start your program EARLY**. Also, sail as often as possible (once a week to be meaningful). Then, as the departure date nears, say within two months or so, begin to taper off, letting your body get adjusted to the fact it will no longer be jogging around a track but will be running in place instead—gym workouts replaced by isometrics while heeling at closehaul. During these two months of switch-over, continue to sail as much as possible, concentrating on preparing your hands, arms and legs for the job that lies ahead.

"Your mental attitude is as important as your physical well-being. In some of the races in which I participated, the reported sightings of objects—not really there, hearing sounds—not really there, were many…too many. It is critical that you be as clear-headed and as adaptable as you possibly can be.

"Your ability, Skipper, to endure under fire must head your critique list, on equal par with your sense of humor and perspective. Ask yourself:

"Could you sail with the pain of a broken rib while still many days from any destination? Could you find the mental know-how to fix the mast if it lost its spreaders? Could you sail efficiently (and for racers, fast) with impaired vision if you lost your glasses? Three singlehanders I had the privilege of knowing had these exact mishaps occur.

"P.S. Please. Don't overreact to what has just been covered, but find a common ground that **YOU** are comfortable with. Not all of the above suggestions will apply to you or your vessel; only YOU can determine what and how much to consider, what and how much to keep, what and how much to discard. You must have faith in yourself, so give yourself that opportunity when it comes your way. It is not often that it does."

Thanks, Gene. Wow.

*4*

### BELOW DECKS BASICS

#### A Cautionary Note About Crew Members

#### The Cabin Itself
*Berths and Bedding—Bric-A-Brac—Bunkboards/Leeboards—Le Head
Lighting—Portholes, Coverings and Screens—Cabin Sole
Stowage Overview—Ventilation—Water Use and Constraints*

#### Things That Work on Board...

#### ... And Things That Don't

#### The Cockpit—Area and Cushions

### *A CAUTIONARY NOTE REGARDING CREW MEMBERS*

Before we discuss the cabin itself, I want to touch on one important item for those of you who plan to have a crew of more than two. YOU, First Mate, are the only one in charge of provisioning and outfitting the vessel with food and other necessary items. To do this, you will be utilizing every bit of space for all pre-planned acquisitions, as well as allotting space for each crew member's gear. *Their gear will be kept in their own bunk.* They **WILL NOT** bring aboard any foodstuffs that cannot be kept in their own quarters. Period.

If you are not firm on this point right from the start, you can get sabotaged with your galley stowage, trying to find room for a month's supply of Horace's guava juice in an already overflowing larder.

The quarters you assign each person are inviolate: It is their space. This should include the bunk of course, with a proper bunkboard/leeboard, their very own hook to hang things on, their very own space for their duffel bag (you have already informed them: no hard-sided suitcases, right?), their own set of towels and a laundry bag (both color-coded), and a way to block out everything and everyone else when trying to sleep. (This can be as simple as a cloth pulled over the bunk opening. Psychologically, it works.) And of course, a light to read by during off-duty hours.

Okay. On to the cabin itself. I could go on for pages on outfitting the basic creature comforts of home, but you already know the ropes, so I will touch but lightly on subjects such as:

### THE CABIN ITSELF

### BERTHS AND BEDDING

Get the best cushions/mattresses you can afford. Use synthetic foam that is firm, lightweight and fire resistant. They should be at least 3" thick. Your back will thank you.

The upholstery is a matter of debate between vinyl and cloth. The former is the most practical, the latter the most handsome. I personally prefer cloth; I cannot **stand** sitting down on cold vinyl! A tweed or a rougher textured fabric helps keep the cushions where they belong and will withstand a lot of wear and tear. Of course, whatever you choose should be easily removable and washable.

Sleeping bags vs. sheets and blankets: Have both available, and let the climate be your guide. In cold waters, tucking into a bag is mighty comforting, in more temperate climes, an open-weave thermal-type blanket fills the bill. Again, just make sure they are washable and fast-drying.

I like flannel sheets. They are not only excellent for cruising in cold weather but in warm they provide a surface which will not get slick from your own perspiration. As to size, vessel bunks 'n' berths are never a true twin-double-queen-king; they are designed to be kittywampus, especially in the V-berth. Suggest you stick to a twin flat (72" x 96"), fold it lengthwise. For a better fit, stitch it across the bottom and 2" up the side.

By the way, if yours is a crew of two, your double bunk will no doubt stay down for the duration. Unless you plan to do laundry while underway, you would be wise to have changes of linen handy: both as the bedding choice and as an extra sheet to tuck into the sleeping bag.

### BRIC-A-BRAC

Keep the decorative items to a minimum. Sure, you want some personalization around, but try not to overdo it. A small picture—macrame over the mast, perhaps.

> *TIP: Handcrafted items encased in a frame behind glass or plastic can bring on mildew and moisture. They are no-go's at sea.*

## BUNKBOARDS/LEEBOARDS

They can be wood, canvas or vinyl. Our main berth is amidships on the port side and our table acts as a leeboard. Just make sure what you choose is installed to last through more than one storm. On the 53-footer we took to Canada, the ones so lovingly sewn by the sailmaster lasted about thirteen minutes into the first squall—he could sail a ship but didn't know diddley about cloth leeboard engineering!

One thing about a leeboard: if designed to block the whole berth from view when in use, the user has an added psychological bonus of privacy.

## LE HEAD

With modern fiberglass construction, most cruising vessels now have a head with reasonable space for the "terlet," basin and additional lockers. Be sure there is a mirror, mounted and well lit, nonmetal rods or hooks for towels, some kind of a soap container, a t.p. holder of sorts and a wastebasket. On "Whither Thou," we use a large plastic baggie for the latter, fastened down with a thumb tack and kept in the opening just below the counter; this puts it at the user's right hand. We also have an inviolate rule: **no** t.p. is flushed down the head. All that does is give one more impetus to a potentially plugged system. Mount this rule over the head of *your* vessel in <u>large print</u>: "NOTHING goes in this receptacle that has not been consumed first by humans. No paper, no pins, no monthlies' trappings—NOTHING!"

With a crew, plastic cups in the head can spread germs. Use paper cups that can be biodegraded with the rest of the paper-type garbage which we will be discussing in Chapter 7.

Store the toilet paper and tissues where they will stay dry. 'Tis discouraging indeed to find a box of tissues and/or a multi pack of t.p., sodden and wasted. How about the bottom of your hanging locker for these items, along with the paper towels and matches?

Oh yes. Speaking of t.p. Stock the one-ply kind only, just in case some does end up in the head.

As for maintenance, have on board a mild abrasive cleaner such as Soft Scrub®, a glass cleaner and a jug of bleach. A half-cup of bleach in the toilet every other day should do it, but **be sure** you do not combine it with any other cleaner and **make sure** you have pumped the head thoroughly first. When bleach meets urine, it creates a noxious gas that has been known to punch a body's lights out. Keep the porthole open (when on the opposite tack) and the whole area should remain socially acceptable.

## *LIGHTING! LIGHTING! LIGHTING!*

I cannot stress too highly the need for the best lighting possible in all work areas aboard. In the galley you need to see into the ice chest; at the nav station, a flashlight doesn't cut it; in the head, toothpaste, shampoo and shaving soap can feel alike in the dark. Got the picture? Then light it well.

Fluorescent fixtures do not draw much juice off the battery and are good supplemental choices. When installing, consider the direction of the beam. Here is where a nav curtain (see below) pays for itself.

Another tip from "Whither Thou": We painted the bulb coverings over the galley and nav station with red nail polish. This provides a "night light" which will not interfere with the helmsman's vision. Your eyes adjust to the dimmed light within seconds.

Consider kerosene lamps. These can be mounted with gimballed fixtures to ensure they will not tip over, they provide a supplemental warm cozy glow to the whole cabin (somewhat hypnotic—not unlike a fireplace), and are easily available from marine chandleries.

### PORTHOLES, COVERINGS AND SCREENS

You will need some kind of covering for the portholes, not only for privacy when dockside, but as a barrier against a too-early sunrise for whoever just came off watch. Most fabric shops carry the marine curtain tracks and tape fasteners. As with the cushions, choose a fabric that is washable and fast drying; an open weave is an excellent choice.

While you are considering porthole coverings, also consider the nav station. A long curtain, when drawn closed, allows the navigator to use his lights without causing night-blindness for the helmsman.

If your portholes actually open, they will need screens; make sure they are tight-fitting and easy to install. In warmer waters, you might want to consider some screening material for the companionway as well.

### THE SOLE OF IT ALL

With sole, as in cabin sole, stick with tradition and go for the teak-and-holly. Fiberglass *is* nonskid, but not only does it look lousy and requires a lot of elbow grease to keep up, it can be downright dangerous if something gets spilled. Forget carpeting: It is a ruddy menace as it absorbs every drop of moisture brought below.

With your teak-and-holly, remove any wax and literally rough up the surface of those areas most used, such as in the front of the galley and the nav station. Always, **SAFETY** first; HOUSEKEEPING second; COSMETIC FEATURES a distant third.

### STOWAGE OVERVIEW

There are those who contend there is never enough stowage space in a small boat. I contend you have more than you think you do, but you do need to take a piercing look at your vessel and be prepared for potential minor surgery.

For instance: On that 53' ketch I keep referring to, we had an amidships bulkhead just over the entrance to the galley: total dead space. Gene and the sailing master took their trusty saws and tools, cut an opening and hinged the door. The result was DRY stowage space for the paper towels, matches, etc.

Does your vessel have either a pilot berth or a quarter berth? How about converting the pilot berth to pure storage by taking out cushions or bedding and installing shelving. Consider using the rear of the quarter berth as heavy-duty storage for lines, charts, spare equipment, etc. It can be compartmentalized with those handy-dandy plastic milk cartons…cut in a top entrance from the cockpit, perhaps? The forward section, more easily accessible, and if it hasn't got one already, could possibly be adapted with some minor surgery to an interior storage locker with lid for navigational aid stowage or the like.

Take a look at your V-berth. Could a hard-plastic single-drawer file cabinet be built in to hold first aid supplies, paper goods, etc?

If you have open shelving on which you hesitate to store things, and it is not feasible to literally build doors to enclose these shelves, trying using bungee cords with small wooden dowels at the top and bottom (as well as in the middle if you have double shelves). The cords can then be "laced" to capture what the shelves hold. This is great for books, tapes, or any light-to-medium-weight supplies.

Use a tape measure and get an experienced and willing carpenter to assist you. Use your shakedown sailing excursions to determine the best use of YOUR total shipboard space.

What it comes down to is: With "x"number of lockers, drawers and areas of stowage aboard, the Skipper will opt for tools, blocks and winch handles, the First Mate will be looking out for cutlery, mittens and galley gear. Work together and divvy it all up as reasonably as you can.

> *TIP: Several small/narrow shelves may suffice better than deep/ wide ones. Use dividers to surround food and dishes securely to keep them from involuntarily co-existing in heavy weather. Fiddled edges on all cutting boards, table top, etc., along with the correct length bungee cords, work marvelously to hold food and dishes in place when heeling.*

> *TIP: (PERHAPS A MAJOR RULE OF THUMB AS WELL?):* **Nothing** *comes aboard that does not have a minimum of two functions. This rule by itself eliminates gadgets and gimmicks. For instance: Take either a footless colander or a strainer, not both. I suggest the latter; it serves more purposes and is more*

*flexible to store. Leave ashore all single-use cookware (e.g., omelet pan) and flatware (e.g., oversized silverplate serving spoons), as well as glass and crystal. These days you can get plastic tumblers and wine glasses that look almost like Waterford. Well, maybe that **is** a bit farfetched, but they do look good, and they don't break or scratch. Consider teak dinner plates instead of china or glass.*

All this does not mean you have to have tunnel vision. On our very first cruise, we took along Piney the Pine Tree, a gift from me to my sea farin' mountain man so the best of his two worlds would always surround him. Piney sits right in the cockpit, or is solidly stashed below as the weather dictated (I can hear Piney now: "Whatinell am I doing on a boat, for cryin' out loud! Why can't I live in a yard, like everyone else?").

So some people sail with pets; we chose a miniature tree. Cleaner.

## *VENTILATION*

Galleys and engines create odors and if they accumulate, they can be nauseating. Suggest you incorporate as **Rule 1:** No smoking allowed below decks. NO EXCEPTIONS. This has nothing to do with personal preference, this has to do with safety. **Rule 2:** Use dorade ventilators to allow air intake without moisture. Turn them to face the current wind direction. **Rule 3:** In warm climates, use a wind scoop on the forward hatch.

## *WATER USE AND CONSTRAINTS*

Install hand or foot pumps to draw water. When you must use force to get every drop, waste is virtually eliminated, and if there is one commodity on a vessel that **cannot** and **must not** be wasted, it's the fresh water supply.

Put in salt water pumps too, both at the galley sink and in the head. In the galley, heated salt water works (really!) for washing the dishes; use your fresh for rinsing only. In the head, the salt water, again heated, can be used for general cleaning.

Do you have a water pressure system? I suppose this is a convenience, but after so many years without, I tend to think of it as an unnecessary luxury. It's just one more mechanical thing that Murphy could screw up, and it could get out of control: If you or your crew take land-based (water-wasting) habits to sea, you may use that water up at an unacceptable rate.

Pressure systems (are perhaps?) worth a second thought in the long run.

As a rule-of-thumb, half a gallon a day per crew member is the rock bottom minimum. A single 45-gallon capacity tank allows no safety margin. Best to have two tanks, each capable of holding at least 30 gallons; one can be the bladder type and one built in. In addition, your total water supply should include a few 3-gallon capacity plastic jury bottles lashed to the safety lines.

### THINGS THAT WORK ON BOARD...

1) Joy® or another bio-degradable liquid detergent. See Chapter 9 for personal hygiene tips using Joy®.

2) Attach a clear plastic hose to your galley faucet at least 2' long; Much easier in a following sea to bring the water to the firmly anchored coffee pot instead of the pot to the water.

3) Velcro® fasteners. Bless the inventor; it saves the day for locker fasteners.

4) Bungee cords. All lengths: from the shortie-of-the-short to at least 1'.

5) Pillows stuffed over any glassware.

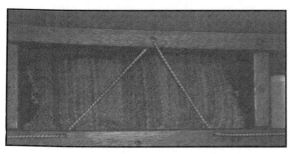

*Protected glassware –*
*Note bungee cord design*

6) Wall cabinet for dishes and flatware.

7) Tupperware® containers. ***USE NO SUBS.***

8) Ziploc® bags. Thickest weight possible; freezer quality at the time of publication is 2 ml. Get the kind that you can label.

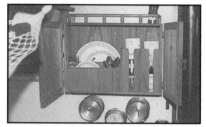

*Wall cabinet for dishes and flatware*

9) Small hammocks. I strung one over the starboard bunk and one between the mast and table pole on port. These are great for storing  matches, gloves, flashlight, medical supplies, fruits and veggies, extra bungee cords…you name it. Get these 100% cotton goodies at a chandlery. Perhaps one or two strung in the V-berth as well?

10) Pencil sharpener mounted at nav station.

11) Rubber bands—large, out-sized—to put around food containers that do not have decent lids of their own. Store these in talcum powder to keep them dry and prevent sticking together.

*One of "Whither's" Hammocks*

12) Towels from the dime store. Bluewater cruising and thick thirsty terry cloth do not marry well. Terry is bulky—terry takes up space even when folded small—worst of all, terry takes **FOREVER** to dry. Get the dime store-type towels, at least two dozen, or get some flour sacks and hem them. A dozen of these cost about the same (or less) than one thick terry cloth towel. An exception to the no-terry rule are the terry fingertip towels; a dozen is great. These do not take up a lot of space (allow one stack space, nominally); they are great for wipe-ups, subbing as bath towels when you ***must have*** "the touch of terry" and also substitute as pot holders. Multi-use, remember!

> *TIP: For all but the fingertips, get pure cotton. Buy the biggest you can get; they might also be used for showers ashore. Since they didn't cost an arm and a leg, it's no big deal if they get left behind.*

13) Curtain at Nav Station.

14) Sponges, both natural and man-made. Dedicate one of each kind to the head, two to the galley, and a <u>large</u> natural-type one for the cockpit.

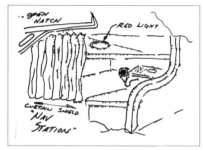

*Curtain at Nav Station*

15) All non-aerosol containers, cleaning products or otherwise. See comment in the next section referring to spray cans.

16) Candles! While ashore or for a becalmed evening. Tall 'n' sturdy or fat 'n' squat. Scented? All. Non drip? Of course.

17) Key mount for wind-up ship's clock.

18) Plastic hangers. Assign one color per crew member.

*Key mount for ship's clock*

19) Cookware—adaptable, more-than-one-use type. Stainless steel is great. Teflon coated? They're okay, too.

20) Fitted cutlery board.

21) Milk cartons, rigid plastic. Put them in the V-berth (or in the head, if there is room) to store soft-skinned fruits and veggies, as well as miscellaneous supplies to have right at hand.

22) Clothespins—**wooden ones**, to fasten laundry and/or drying towels to the lifelines.

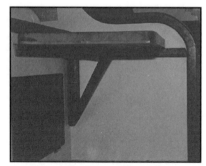

*Fitted cutlery board on "Whither Thou"*

23) Sierra cups instead of muffin tins. These are available at any camping or backpack outlet. Not only do these meet the "more than one purpose" rule of thumb by eliminating the single-use muffin tins, but the muffins are bigger and better. Takes a bit longer to bake— so what's five minutes or so?

24) Stereo speakers mounted in over-a-bunk locker doors. Good resonance! Convert existing phonograph records and CD's to tape cassettes, and have extra stereo system batteries on hand.

*Locker door mounted stereo speakers*

### ...AND THINGS THAT DON'T

*"Our life is frittered away by detail...simplify, simplify!"*                    *— Thoreau*

1) Plastic egg cartons sold in chandleries. They pop open and flip over in the ice chest. Do not believe the labels.

2) Finger-sized locker fasteners that forever lose their eeny weeny teeny tiny never-to-be-found-again spring. Naturally, it will be when you are at 30° heel and all the dishes are falling, not to mention the flour, the sugar...

3) Mouse-sized entries on amply wide lockers. Why do they **do** this??? Cut these doors wide, cut 'em tall and use outside locker hooks. You may not like their looks, but I guarantee, the first heel when the locker door flies open and stores are all over the sole, you will forever change your "cosmetic" priorities.

*Larger door/
Greater access*

4) To save $$$, look elsewhere than in a chandlery for: binoculars, flashlights, stainless steel hardware. These items do not need an expensive marine label, they just have to be stainless steel and/or waterproof.

5) Off-brand plastic freezer containers.

6) Spray cans. All spray cans. Learn to live without hair spray and get cleaning supplies in a non-aerosol form. Spray cans seize and rust fast, their odors can be nauseating in a small vessel, and they can really louse up the cabin wood surfaces.

7) Scrub pads with metal in them. That eliminates several popular brands right off the top. Stick to the sponge type.

8) Extensive multiple furniture waxes, et al. A can of teak oil, a soft cloth…does wonders and does the job.

9) Anything silver or silverplate. Both get discolored and pitted from the salt air.

10) Hangers with metal rods. They will rust every time.

11) One-of-a-kind cookware, e.g., an omelet pan, or cast iron cookware. The latter is too heavy and it rusts.

12) As mentioned already, thick-heavy, heavy-thick luxury towels, and clothespins with metal springs.

### COCKPIT—AREA AND CUSHIONS

Your cockpit area serves a twofold purpose and therefore is worth a word or three while considering "basics."

When you are underway, especially if the weather is brisk, or during sail changes when a jumble of lines abound, keep the clutter out of sight. Cushions, eyeglasses—any loose gear—can be swept away in frenzied seas or winds. Rule: If it ain't tied down, store it below.

But…when at anchor or when the seas and winds are calm, the cockpit becomes a sun room or, if you will, a patio (especially if you have a dodger!) Then it's time to haul out the cushions (Coast Guard approved, naturally) and enjoy.

A note on cockpit cushions: Some vessels are equipped with custom-fitted ones; they are comfy and attractive to look at—while dockside or in calm waters. But they become a downright nuisance when cruising, especially if those seas and winds get aggressive. Because of their length you have storage problems, and of course you cannot just leave them in the cockpit to get soaked or blown overboard.

Think these through carefully, please.

# 5

## *PERSONAL GEAR*

*"Appearances are often deceiving."*                                        — *Aesop*

### *THE GO'S AND THE NO GO'S*

Slick yachting and boat magazines just love displaying illustrations of the First Mate, lounging sexily on deck and dressed—either to the nines or just barely.

Great for shoreside maybe, but underway it's a different story.

At sea and generally speaking, dungarees, shorts and jeans will be your best and most comfortable friends, along with sweaters, sweaters and more sweaters: lightweight pullovers (100% cotton or lightweight wool) as well as heavy duty wool ones.

You will need shoes, both deck and lightweight canvas. You will need caps: wool for winter, sun visors or brimmed hats for summer's sun protection. You will need mittens, weatherproof jackets and pants for cold. You'll want bikinis, halters and shorts for tropical climates.

*These* will be the mode of the day.

For bluewater detail, pay special attention to the shoes you select. Nonskid soles—white, please!—are a must. (Black soles leave all sorts of scuff marks on the deck and cabin sole.) Incorporate a no-bare-feet rule and extend it to include thongs and/or strapless sandals (except for shore patrol).

As to foul-weather gear, get the best you can afford. They do cost, but with any kind of luck they should last for a few years and/or cruises or both. Ask around for recommendations from your sailing friends; this is a subject that generates as many opinions as you have friends, and the price tag does not always reflect the best quality. Be sure the gear is in a size to fit over your regular outer bulky clothing.

> *I personally recommend pants and jacket for the First Mate, leaving the bib overalls to the Captain. The latter is a royal pain when nature calls. If you must have overalls for yourself, replace any fasteners/buttons with Velcro®; it will make the head trip a bit more comfortable and speedier! Face it: If you are wearing foul-weather gear in the first place, you're needed topside, not down below.*

When considering shore clothes to take along, use common sense. A pair of trim slacks, a cotton dress, blouse and cardigan will for you in most cases suffice. Keep a jacket, tie and a pair of dress slacks for him to cover the visits to yacht clubs and/or restaurants during ports of call.

Whatever you elect to take on shore and en route, make sure they are fast-drying and do not require a lot of storage space. Use wool for warmth (even wet wool is better than polyester in rotten seas), choose pure cotton for tropical climes, have one or two changes of everything and one feminine outfit for shore, including those don't-use-on-board sexy sandals.

Accessories? One word covers it: forget it. Okay, two words. Jewelry has no place on a boat. Well, if you must, stash a pair of earrings, a bracelet and a necklace in your private drawer. But please! Save them for shore time. Aboard a vessel a ring, bracelet or necklace could cause more than a sore finger, wrist or neck—what with deck gear awash, sheets fouled and flying. UNCLUTTERED immediate reactions are needed **now**.

To every rule there is an exception, and to the above no-accessory one the exception being eye glass sport strap(s). These are vital, and sometimes it is necessary for you as the First Mate to either provide or see to it that your crew member get them. See your optometrist for these and make sure *they are used*. One for each set of specs (shades or otherwise) is a lot less expensive than replacing the pair that just went overboard.

> *Believe it, this is expensive experience talking—our optometrist told us that sailors (including us) are his best customers!*

To wrap it up, where you will be cruising will naturally determine the main gist of gear. If hot 'n' tropical, you will no doubt tuck in extra swimwear, cover-ups, and big brimmed hats that fold. If cold is your destination, there will be more long-sleeved tops, long johns, wool socks, foul weather boots, wool mitties and gloves and…yeah, water-proof ones too, for when you are handling wet gear and lines. Tuck in wool scarfs to wear under the foul weather jacket to catch raindrops.

With real cold, there are the down-filled vests, pants and jackets. Why do you want to get THAT cold?

*6*

***SAFETY BELOW***

*"What we anticipate seldom occurs; what we least expect generally happens."*
**— Disraeli**

S ailing through a gale on any size of vessel is a chore; on a small vessel it's down right wearisome. You will call on every bit of energy, vigor, endurance and chutz pah just to execute the simplest function. But first and foremost, you **must,** mate, *consider your own safety*.

Move carefully, with deliberate caution within the cabin.

Use the handrails at every step.

There is an inviolate ship rule: One hand is for you, the other hand is for the ship. Apply this rule always.

It is stowage, or lack of it, that causes the majority of your belowdecks boating household accidents. On shore the kitchen was where those nasty accidents most often occurred. Now you've added motion, lots of it, so encase and trap everything: utensils, heavy tools, sharp tools…these should have permanent and dedicated stowage space. Knives, cutlery…anything with a sharp edge or point needs protection. For them, *and for you*.

Secure locker doors to keep them from flying open and smashing against hands or feet when the vessel lurches.

Make sure the companionway is kept clear, both to provide uncluttered passage as the Skipper/Navigator constantly recheck their instruments, and to bring in as much ventilation as possible into the cabin.

Do not allow crew members to block the companionway and do not use it yourself, unless you are handing up dinner and even then, step lively.

The gimballed stove is vital for bluewater cruising, but in super heavy or rotten seas, it *can* become your enemy. Guard it with a stainless steel bar so neither cook nor crew get thrown into it, and *make sure the fastening pin is in position.*

Never ever forget the cook's safety. Design or buy a cookstrap that can be efficiently mounted in YOUR vessel, no matter what the galley configuration is. Here again, your sailmaker may be of help. Most straps are made of sturdy webbing goods: you "sit" against it and it is secured on each side with snap hooks to eyebolts. See to it that it is installed at **YOUR** hip level, mate.

(Or, as commented before, if all else fails, use the Skipper!)

One more thing to remember: **no. bare. feet. in. galley. EVER!** You do not need spilled hot coffee on your tootsies, nor do you need a flying frying pan to crush exposed toes. Always always **ALWAYS**—wear some kind of protective foot cover in the galley. Promise?

Safety down below—are we still in the galley?—also means keeping something on hand to douse a sudden fire flare-up. Firstly, keep the area over and immediately around the stove top clean of such potential inflammables as curtains, towels and paper goods— particularly paper towels that often lay their own path due to an open and breeze-filled companionway.

The Skipper and you will have already determined how many and what kind of fire extinguishers are to be kept throughout the vessel. Make sure one of them is in the galley. And for Pete's sake, **KNOW HOW TO USE IT!** The best one, with today's technology, is the Halon.

If you have chosen an alcohol stove, you will be priming it a lot. Keep a teapot of water handy for this step in case of fire flare-up. I nearly burned up Gene's first vessel— while we were first dating, yet!—because I was such a nerd about precautions. Boy, almost destroying a guy's boat can really threaten to put a crimp in the relationship! In those days, there was no Halon. That antiquated powder-type extinguisher made such a MESS.

Alcohol fires can come about due to flawed fuel, incorrect priming, or if the stove itself went south for the winter. But the fire *looks* worse than it *is,* really. A reasonable amount of water usually takes care of it, *if* the temperature of the burning material can be lowered by spraying it with water. Remember this basic: ***do not spread it.***

Naturally, no matter what type your stove, be it butane, propane or CNG:

1)  **Turn off the safety valves between use.**

2)  **A fire or ignition of leaking fuel is an instant hazard**.

3)  **Use the Halon immediately and get the crew the hell away from the area!**

Better still, practice all safety rules and never need to refer to the above.

*TIP: With a kerosene stove, for God's sake,* **DON'T use water***. Smother it (with a damp towel), or use the Halon.*

*Whither Thou's Galley, At Rest*

*7*

*THE GALLEY: AN OVERVIEW IN NO PARTICULAR ORDER*

*Stoves and Fuel*

*Galley Sinks*

*Refrigeration Systems*

*Counterspace*

*Garbage Detail*

*"Put all your eggs in one basket—and watch that basket."*                    *— Mark Twain*

In the next chapter, we will be concentrating in detail on how to find and use space in this vital part of the vessel. But since the galley is the center of all activity, as is the kitchen on land, I have given it this space of its own to cover some basic equipment and fixture considerations.

One thing about the galley, you will never be lonely: No matter where yours is located, you are always right in the middle of the action!

## *STOVES AND FUEL*

Be sure you fully understand your stove; it is nothing like the ones on land. Be it alcohol, propane, butane, kerosene or CNG, each stove has advantages, each has disadvantages. Best to look at all of them in detail, if you are still in the purchasing mode, and determine what your priorities are.

For instance, alcohol and kerosene are inexpensive and easily obtained anywhere in the world, but take forever to heat up and create dirt and offensive odor, respectively. They also require a second fuel for priming.

Our first alcohol stove took over a half hour to get the coffee water boiling; B-O-R-I-N-G. The kerosene replacement nearly drove us back to land with the gawdawful mess it made in the galley when it decided to flare up, which was all the time. It smelled horrible, too.

Propane is fast and relatively economical, but if a leak develops **you don't smell it!** The fumes sink to the bilge and—with a lighted match—that's all she wrote, folks. For this reason, propane tanks **MUST** be stored topside, in their own protective containers.

CNG (Compressed Natural Gas): Somewhat expensive to replace the tanks but it is *lighter* than air. If a leak does develop, CNG goes up and out, not down and in. To me and mine, that is more than worth the price. Therefore, our personal current choice is our 3-burner-with-an-oven CNG. (I cannot see us changing this choice unless we settle in an area where CNG is not available). Although this baby takes up more space in the galley, uses large amounts of fuel, and has an oven that can overheat the cabin in the summer, in my opinion it is the smallest you should consider for reasonably efficient and varied cooking capability—and to offer a warm muffin on a cold morning.

But—those are *our* current priorities, gained through some expensive learning experiences. Yours could be different. Ask opinions of your boating friends who own each kind. See what they have to say, then…read…read…read!!

There are other ways to cook besides using the galley; I am referring to having a charcoal grill aboard. Of course this is only for use when in port or at anchor, never for use on the high seas unless you are totally becalmed, but they are popular. There is a marine version designed to fit into the flag socket on the stern, and using it helps keep the cabin cool on hot days.

> *Tips for using "The Barby": Avoid too much priming, have a water container handy, use long-handled implements and wear gloves. Store in a sturdy bag (canvas or ripstock nylon) and, since it is metal, keep it the hell away from the compass!*

## GALLEY SINKS

These serve many uses. Obviously, the most important is to fix the meals and wash the dishes. But while under a rough way, they also store the pot or pan, the cups, plates and glasses just used, or soon to be used. In addition, it is the only place to keep the thermos of hot beverage and the night watch snacks (which we will discuss in the next chapter) for immediate access by the on-watch crew person. I even read somewhere that one first mate scrubbed the sink out and then kneaded her bread dough in it. Oooh kay.

Make sure the aforementioned sink is deep enough to hold dishes and pans safely, but also be prepared to find eyeglasses, goggles, gloves, caps 'n' hats, a just-used flashlight, binocs, beer cans (both empty and half-full), live crab—you name it. This is why those handy hammocks are suggested (no no no! Not for the crab! But for the eyeglasses, the gloves, the caps, the flashlight….)

Beware the wide but shallow sink that looks so great…until with the motion of the vessel, the water is up and over the edge. They are strictly for show, not for blow.

## REFRIGERATION SYSTEMS

The ice chest need not be large to be efficient, but it should have first class insulation, be top loading with a lid you can secure while opened, have a screened drain, and be no deeper than *you* can reach. There are also those mobile types that operate AC/DC; they work off the boat battery while cruising and plug into the electrical outlet when dockside. These are super, but again, take heed of priorities. Anything that operates off the battery can cause power failure, sometimes just when it is needed most elsewhere. Or, it can necessitate carrying an extra generator. If this is your priority for comfortable sailing, fine. But you *can* do without, as you will see in the next chapter.

## COUNTERSPACE

So you don't have eleventy-five feet of tile surrounding you. Who needs it? With efficient arrangement and using Sam's quote (see below), your sub-compact counterspace will do quite nicely, thank you. For supplemental space, consider another tip from "Whither Thou": We have a cutting board that mounts just the other side of the galley bulwark; with fiddles, it becomes my cutting/serving/all-purpose surface. It is fitted to go on the stove top when we are in rough seas. Also on our vessel, the galley is on the starboard side at the foot of the companionway ladder, so I use the ladder as I need it (stacking dishes, etc.) when it is not being used in its rightful way.

*"A place for everything and everything in its place."*                    **— Samuel Smiles**

*GARBAGE DETAIL*

Use only paper bags for recyclable garbage collected at sea; these dissolve when jettisoned. (Believe me, when you get through provisioning the galley, you'll have *plenty* of paper bags!) Plastic bags should be used ONLY to store crushed garbage destined for disposal on shore. Please do not litter the surface of the sea: tin cans with one end removed make a neat home for some hermit crab down below.

The stuff being kept for shore disposal can be stored in the stern lazaret or topside; if the latter, be sure to secure it tightly.

As a rule of thumb, discard at sea: **GLASS OR METAL CONTAINERS**, taking one end off the metal, or filling with water so they will sink; **PAPER THAT HAS NOT BEEN TREATED IN ANY WAY; RAW REFUSE** from your galley such as meats, shells from the crab, veggie and fruit trims (cut up a bit).

Keep for shore disposal: **anything plastic** (includes plastic bags, **all styrofoam-type products); all paper that has been treated and waxed**, such as dairy containers.

OKAY. We have now touched on just about everything in both the basics and generalities departments. Time to get down to brass tacks and get this show on the road!

## *8*

### THE REAL AND WORKABLE GALLEY

*Step 1: Inventory and the Staple List*

*Step 2: Menus:*
*Preliminary Suggestions—Night Watch Food—Menu Planning*
*Summary—Menu Ideas for the First Bumpy Days*

*Step 3: The Shopping List*

*Step 4: Shopping and Storing:*
*Staples—Pre-Cooked Meal Ingredients—Perishables—Fresh Foodstuffs to Consider—*
*Foods for Immediate Use—Nutritional and High Energy Supplements*

*Summary*

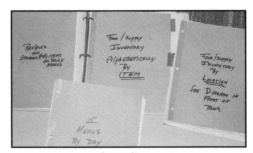

*The Infamous Notebook—*                           *—and Its Componets*

No matter what the size of your vessel, there is a common denominator when provisioning for bluewater cruising. You, smart one, have figured that out by now: The trick is to design a blueprint of thorough pre-planning and preparation. As before, apply the suggestions that follow to *your* vessel, adapting to the number of mouths *you* will be feeding and what you will have to cook with…and in. (This latter will be anything from the basic minimum such as an alcohol [or] kerosene stove and ice chest, to the maximum that might include full freezer/fridge, 3-burner-with-oven stove, and maybe a microwave oven thrown in for good measure).

No matter what equipment you choose, there are four steps to follow, with shopping being the last. Plan to put in a minimum of one week preliminary groundwork before going near a supermarket. Two weeks would be more realistic. So, get a sturdy 3-ring binder, plenty of paper, some sharp pencils and good erasers. Here we go!

### STEP 1: INVENTORY AND THE STAPLE LIST

Take a complete inventory of what is already on board, both food and supplies. These items will be the beginning of your menu work-ups and staple list. Make a note of what you have served your Skipper and/or crew that has been especially well received. Also, ask for and list those foods your crew members either cannot or will not eat due to allergies or perhaps violent dislikes.

As you inventory and prepare these first guidelines, list WHAT you have, HOW MUCH and WHERE it is located. Draw some charts showing all the storage areas and label them. For instance, the compartments under the V-berth could be "Locker No. 1," storage under the port settee, "Locker 2," cupboards over the starboard settee, "Locker 3." Refer to Appendix D, showing both the layout of our vessel and the 53' ketch to which I have been referring, for possible ideas to apply to your vessel.

Look for usable dead space (such as the face-lift described in Chapter 4, "Stowage/ Overview"). Do not overlook the shower ceiling if you have a shower. Give these areas a hinged entrance and voila!—additional dry storage. Also, don't forget the bottom of the hanging locker found on nearly every vessel; as I've said before, this is often the best place for paper towels, toilet paper, matches and the like.

From your newly-created master chart, generally determine what each storage area will contain. Assign a *separate page* in your binder for *each storage area*. The storage areas nearest the galley should hold those foodstuffs and supplies you plan to use every day, leaving the larger areas farthest away from the galley to hold all bulk goods.

List your current inventory, then begin your basic staples list with those BULK supplies you know you will use: favorite spices, sugar, flour, instant rice, paper towels, napkins, safety matches, flashlight batteries, etc.

If yours is a virgin boat, this list will be a long one.

## STEP 2: MENUS

D raw up **ITEMIZED** menus for two or three meals a day plus daytime snacks, for 14 days, balancing for both variety and nutrition. (We find lunch to be our least "cooking" meal, so we plan breakfast and dinner, with the midday snack consisting of fruit, cheese and crackers only). However, your crew's habits must determine how many meals per day you will plan.

See Appendix A for menu suggestions.

*Your cruise is longer than 14 days? Start over at the beginning.*

## *PRELIMINARY SUGGESTIONS*

Plan breakfast so that egg consumption is alternated with an eggless meal such as hot cereal with fruit; cold cereal with warmed canned peaches and hot muffins; or melon slices and pancakes. Pay close attention to breakfast; it is often the favorite meal of the day.

Preliminary suggestions for dinners: a pasta-based dinner one night (spaghetti, or linguine and canned clams) could be followed the next day with a meat or fish dinner (canned, freeze-dried or that fish you just caught), enhanced with a cabbage salad and freshly baked bread (more about those two items shortly). The next night, try fried rice with chicken bits (again canned or freeze-dried), the next night a hearty soup, using the 3-minute oriental-type with noodles but augmented with last night's leftovers…or perhaps a fish chowder (again fresh or canned) served with biscuit-mix drop biscuits.

Beginning to get the idea?

By pre-planning every menu item and detail, you eliminate having cold cereals four mornings in a row, running out of bacon a week into the trip, or not even having bacon or the biscuit mix on board.

As you make out each menu, think through the ingredients, adding any missing ones to your staples list. Do you usually add parsley to your spaghetti sauce? Then add parsley flakes to your list, along with the Parmesan cheese. And don't forget the Chianti!

## *A NOTE ON NIGHT WATCH FOODSTUFFS*

While we are on the subject of staples, include a totally separate list—and have a totally separate storage space—for night watch food supplies. These should be high in energy, high in protein, and HANDS OFF during the day. Package them in one-night units. Once that night's supply is gone, it is gone, no dipping into tomorrow's supply.

Suggested night watch food: Individual-sized/wrapped chocolate bars and packages of salted peanuts; granola bars; trail mix (which you can make up yourself with raisins, regular-roasted peanuts—not dry roasted as they do not combine well with other ingredients—chocolate chips, sunflower seeds, etc). Include individual tea bags, both regular and herbal (tea laced with honey is pure energy). Include individual packets of hot chocolate above and beyond the daytime alloted amount.

A mug of hot cocoa and a candy bar is just the ticket when either coming off the midnight watch, or about to go on at 0400.

*TIP: Consider storing some foods, such as daytime snacks and nightwatch foods, in a waterproof container in the cockpit itself, for when the weather is outrageous. This works, too, for fruit juices needed to offset dehydration.*

## MENU PLANNING SUMMARY

Keep in mind these two absolutes:

1) A minimum of one hot meal per day is mandatory for the health of the crew;

2) *Their health determines both the safety and the pleasure of the passage.*

Quality of the meals aboard is among the most important factors on any vessel, rating right up there with the competence of the Skipper and the savvy of the navigator. **Do not** let anyone undermine your importance in this arena, mate!

Gene tells the story of a mountain expedition which failed just short of the summit, due to poor food pre-planning: all they had left were desserts. In those altitudes, you simply cannot exist, let alone continue climbing on lemon pudding alone. It's the same at sea: I don't care how rotten the seas, how fierce the winds, or how seasick some may be, the rest of the crew still has to eat, and eat well.

## THOSE FIRST BUMPY DAYS

Those first few days out can be violent…violent seas, violent winds and some crew members wondering: What am I DOING out here? We here on the Pacific Coast know that the first three days out are among the roughest you can encounter. Until uniform seas are reached, with all that pitching and rolling going on, the cook isn't about to do any serious cooking.

Have meals for those first three days utilize prepared foods which require the addition of boiling water **only**: e.g., instant soup mixes, instant cocoa or hot chocolate in individual packets, instant oatmeal, etc. Should the cook—you—be the one to experience the *mal de mer,* the Skipper or another crew member can easily take over supervising these basic arrangements.

The last thing at night and again first thing in the morning, boil fresh water, fill your <u>push top thermos</u>, DESIGNED FOR HOT FOODS—that doesn't have to be opened and takes only fingertips to operate— and prop it up in the sink. Keep the container holding all instant foods readily available—the "cooking" is done.

In addition, have available fresh fruit sections, tomato juice, *diluted* citrus juices (pure grapefruit or orange can be a bit hard on a queasy system), dried fruits, and soft-boiled eggs.

### STEP 3: THE SHOPPING LIST

Start your list from the menus you have just finished and your now-lengthy staples list. Again, if yours is a virgin boat, be prepared to spend money. When we outfitted the ketch to Canada on her maiden voyage, the cost of the spices and condiments alone made me swallow twice, but I knew better than to eliminate any item. Well-balanced, *tasty* meals are so vital; a touch of more than salt and pepper to a can of stew makes all the difference in the world (try a smattering of parsley and/or vegetable flakes, some reconstituted dried onion, a dusting of thyme and basil, a touch of Worcestershire sauce and some burgundy wine thrown in for good measure).

To determine the quantity to buy of each item, apply basic mathematics: List how many times in the expected passage duration you plan to serve eggs, for example. Multiply that total by the number of crew and add those required for cooking or baking. Apply the same math to all ingredients in every meal; e.g., bacon slices, pasta servings, 2-crew-per-each-soup-mix packages, cans of meat or fish, apples—per person, per lunch,, per snack—etc.

As for bulk staples (such as butter and/or margarine for both table and cooking, paper towels, toilet paper, etc.), I follow a basic rule of thumb: ONE UNIT (pound, package, roll) for each TWO crew members PER WEEK. To the final total, I add one extra for good measure.

Regarding the night watch food supplies: Plan two or three snacks per crew member per watch, one going on, one going off, with a possible midwatch snack as well. Example: For 2 snacks apiece for 2 crew members on each watch, with a total of 3 watch segments (2100-2400, 0000-0300, 0300-0600). 2x2x3, or 6 crew members x 2 snacks each = 12 snack per night. Multiply by 14 nights. Total: 168 items for a 2-week cruise, and each night's packet contains 12 items.

## STEP 4: SHOPPING AND STORING

Finally! Now you are ready to tackle the supermarket, but hold it—not everything at once!

Plan three separate trips:

FIRST: All those staples and most menu ingredients;

THEN: Menu ingredients for any pre-cooking and freezing;

LAST: All perishables.

### STAPLES

Since this will be the largest and the most expensive category, your local market manager will just adore you, and should be the first person you seek out. Let him/her know what you are about and ask where to park each grocery cart as you fill it up (there will be three or four). Ask too, about bulk discounts; some give 2% to 5% off the top, and every little bit helps. At the very least you should luck out with your own checkout stand and favorite cashier!

Just buying and carting all that stuff back to the vessel is enough for one day. Leave the storing until tomorrow.

Next day, begin by re-packaging. No cardboard boxes of rice, sugar or salt, please, unless you *like* massive messy cleanup chores en route, not to mention wasted supplies. Therefore, part of your staple supplies should include lots of the grip-closed type HEAVY DUTY plastic freezer bags, two boxes of 20 each minimum, plus one more for use en route. Again I suggest Ziploc® freezer quality of 2.7 mils thick; the thinner ones just don't do the job. ***Double-bag*** all bulk-sized items such as salt, rice, flour, corn-meal, etc.

You can also use various sizes of plastic freezer containers that are truly airtight. Again, Tupperware®. The best of two worlds is utilizing both.

Next, start storing your treasures. ***Record each item as you put it away*** on those inventory lists and charts you make back at Step. No. 1, remember? This is essential: It is much too easy to forget where you stashed that needed can of stewed tomatoes. This is particularly true if more than one person will be doing the cooking or, as in my experience, with the male racers doing their thing sans the Planning Lady.

I have found it most efficient to make up two complete inventories:

1) **STORAGE AREA** listing "what" and "how much"
   e.g., Locker A: 1-5# canned ham, 3-2# canned hams;

2) **INDIVIDUAL ITEM, ALPHABETIZED,** e.g., under
   "H" is Ham, 1-5#  Locker A; 3-2# Hams, Locker A; Hamburger
   Relish, Galley Locker #2.

See Appendix C for a suggested "road map."

Yes, it **is** double the work—now. But you have the time now, as well as the available markets. You won't have either once out at sea. This method totally erases the frustration once underway, when the cook for the day knows just where to go to find the applesauce (listed under "A" in the second inventory) to go with one of those canned hams (listed under "H" and the main item for dinner).

> *TIP: Include recipes in your binder and cross-reference the menus*
> *accordingly. Guarantees your own off-watch undisturbed slumber!*
> *See Appendix B.*

### PRE-COOKED MEAL INGREDIENTS

Pre-cooking and freezing anything depends, of course, on your galley. With no refrigeration other than the ice chest, this step was all but eliminated for "Whither Thou." But if yours is a fully equipped galley, as was the ketch we both sailed to Canada and Gene skippered to Hawaii, you may elect to fry up a few chickens and/or fill some plastic containers with homemade stew, soups, or what-have-you.

If so, this will be the basis of your next market onslaught: to buy foodstuffs you can **buy, cook, freeze, wrap, label clearly, then store aboard j**ust prior to departure. As you put the frozen packages away, LIST, in your handy-dandy notebook , WHAT GOES IN THE FREEZER **AND** THE ORDER IN WHICH IT GOES. Load from the bottom up, storing the most distant day on the bottom: Day #14, Day #9, Day #5, etc. When the first day arrives that everyone is on their physical feet, the first real meal is right on top. See end of Appendix C.

### PERISHABLES

Sorry, there is no way to do this one in advance. Get all the dairy products, fresh vegetables, fresh fruits and salad makings **no sooner than** the day before departure.

Those open air hammocks mentioned before work great for these items, either strung in the main cabin, the V-berth section or in the aft cabin if you have one. On our own vessel the two ham- mocks in the main cabin hold a month's supply of fresh foodstuffs.

*TIP: Don't store fresh veggies or fruits in plastic bags; the foods rot faster.*

*TIP: Do* NOT *keep* **soft-skinned** *fruits or veggies in these other- wise indispensable hammocks. I bought over $6.00 worth of gor- geous peaches for our trip north with a crew of nine; not one darn peach was enjoyed. After two days of our infamous Pacific Coast offshore weather and seas, with the hammock constantly slamming into both hatch cover and bulkhead, we had peach purée all over*

*the main cabin sole. I had a slippery dangerous mess to clean up—
and a very red face. As suggested before, store those soft-skinned
beauties in your plastic milk cartons set in the V-berth or in the
shower stall.*

*TIP: Lettuce does not keep at all, so get only enough for a day or
two. Rely instead on cabbage for your salads, both the green and the
red variety; they keep up to a month in those hammocks. And using
cabbage does not mean constant cole slaw: tear the cabbage just as
you would lettuce, add fresh or reconstituted onion, canned shoestring beets, some croutons...toss with either oil and vinegar or
build a sour cream dressing from a packet of dry mix. Luscious! Or,
for a* **really** *Far Out dressing, see Appendix B.*

## FRESH FOODSTUFFS TO CONSIDER

These travel well and will keep for at least three weeks if kept dry and in as cool a
spot as possible: melons (still ripening); grapes, lemons, limes, oranges and grapefruits;
onions (all varieties except green); garlic; apples; cucumbers, peppers (green, red and
yellow, though the yellow ones will not last as long); zucchini, other squashes and beets;
bananas and tomatoes if you purchase them while green to ripen en route; baking potatoes; red potatoes; eggplant; the cabbage, of course; bulk cheeses; bulk lunch meats,
and eggs.

Eggs. There are so many suggestions of how to buy and then to store. I buy mine at
the supermarket and have yet to have one go bad on me. I would *like* to get freshly laid
ones, unwashed and unrefrigerated as so many suggest, but there are no farms nearby. As
for coating them, I have never been too keen on smearing a lot of petroleum jelly on
something I plan to cook later. Just make sure they are stored below the vessel's water
level; they'll be fine.

I mentioned bulk cheese and lunch meats. When buying in this manner, you
end up spending a lot less than getting regular sized packages of cheese and bologna
in the supermarket. Go to a cheese shop, buy a whole cheese and you might get
another discount.

Smoked gouda and smoked cheddar travel extremely well with no refrigeration whatsoever. If a little mold appears, wipe if off with a cloth dipped in white vinegar. The mold comes off slick and neat and there is no lingering vinegary taste on the cheese. I am told this is how the deli people keep their displays fresh.

Ask *your* deli person for recommendations on lunch meats; on "Whither Thou" we favor a summer sausage.

### FOODS FOR IMMEDIATE USE

I have experienced minimal success with storing carrots (surprisingly) and celery, as well as leaf veggies, radishes, mushrooms and green salad onions. These should be used up within the first few days.

### NUTRITIONAL AND HIGH ENERGY SUPPLEMENTS

For nutritional concerns, especially if you are planning an extremely long passage, a few additions should be part of the pre-planning. To the cheeses already mentioned, add: nuts, rice, macaroni, beans, lentils, cereals (granola and/or wheat germ), margarine (in stick form), more eggs…and dried fruits, for when the fresh stuff is gone and also for anyone who gets a tummy block.

Protein can be supplied by using powdered or canned milk, *salted* butter, fresh eggs, and meats that have been canned, smoked, salted or dried. Also, remember those fish you **are going** to catch!

As for high energy, we have already talked about night watch food which should give an ample supply of energy. However, if you want additional supplies to those suggested, consider cake mixes, instant or canned puddings, additional candy, and bread for carbohydrate supplements.

*SUMMARY*

Basically, there you have it. You have put in approximately one to two weeks of pre-planning effort that will pay off in spades. Good going, Mate!

More thoughts and suggestions to keep in mind:

...If you do not have a refrigeration system, consider the merits of dry ice which can be obtained from a fishing/sports outlet. Dry ice usually comes in sheets as opposed to blocks, and is normally wrapped in newspaper. Handle with care and DO NOT let it touch your skin! Place on top of your regular ice. *Depending on the quality of your ice chest insulation, dry ice can last a couple of weeks, so it is certainly worth considering for long passages.*

...If weight and/or rock-bottom minimum stowage space is the primary concern, you may elect to utilize the freeze-dried foods found at your local camping/backpacking supply center. There is virtually no weight involved and, with a little ingenuity, they can be made fairly tasty. They do cost, though, and this can be a real challenge to your budget. Instead of relying on them as your main source of food, consider using the freeze-dried chicken or meats for an occasional change of pace. This also applies to those off-the-shelf convenience foods which require no refrigeration and are meant for the microwave. Again, they are expensive if purchased for many meals, and not quite as tasty as the endorsements might suggest.

...Some baking will need to be done en route. No matter how much freezer/refrig space you have, there is simply no way to carry enough fresh or frozen bread products. In Appendix B, I have included some bread recipes that require no perishables and are simple to prepare, as well as beer bread—ridiculously easy and soooo good!  If there is nuthin' better than messing about in boats, it's even better messin' around with a hunk of fresh bread in hand, hot from the oven! *If you do plan to purchase bakery products, make sure the breads are double-wrapped and unsliced. Fruit breads and cakes will last but they have a tendency to mold; frozen cakes and pies create potential health hazards if they have creamed fillings.*

*TIP: English muffins keep fairly well, so you may elect to put in a few packages, but be sure to store them in a dry place. "Dry" is NOT under the refrigerator shelf. When the generator goes unused for a couple of days and things begin to drip, guess where the water goes. Soggee.*

…Put in a few cans of the 7-oz size Mexican hot sauce. You can find this in the Mexican foods section of your supermarket. This is great to dress up tired food or add a zingy touch to an otherwise bland dish. See the recipe for Slumgullion in Appendix B which illustrates what I mean.

…For the diet-conscious sailor, turn your vessel into a forced fat farm, if that's your bag. Once the mooring lines are cast off, what you have on board is IT: no sneaky bag of potato chips to taunt and tempt!

*If cholesterol levels are your concern, choose soft (not stick) marga-rine with a zero cholesterol level. Ditto mayonnaise and any other dairy product. Use only nonfat or lowfat powdered milk. When baking, and eggs are called for, use either powdered eggs or the egg substitutes found in the dairy section of the supermarket, or substi-tute two egg whites for each whole egg needed. Regarding these last two suggestions, obviously the egg substitutes take up the least amount of storage space, and should be kept as cool as possible.*

*A further word about cholesterol levels: A lifestyle containing consistent activity and excercise (such as sailing!) uses up choles-terol just as it does calories. So, more intake of both the "good" and the "not so good" cholesterol types will not be as detrimental to your system while at sea as they might be on land in passive activi-ties. You might want to check with your doctor for his recommenda-tions of foods to consider in moderation, those to avoid completely, and those to use freely.*

…Even if you will not be maintaining a diet-restrictive galley, have at least part of your powdered milk supply the nonfat or lowfat variety. Some of the recipes in Appendix B call for the nonfat kind.

…When selecting canned goods, get the best quality. There is positively no room on a boat for second-rate food products of any kind, but this is *especially* true with canned goods. Do not buy dented or rusty cans and NEVER any that bulge or leak!

> *Choose the smaller-sized cans whenever possible. I know six of the 4-oz will cost more than two of the 12-oz, but there is virtually no place to store open containers of anything. If you choose the size of cans that will be consumed at one meal, you will have less mess to worry about.*

…I cannot emphasize this enough: **DO NOT LET OTHERS TALK YOU OUT OF YOUR PREPARATIONS**. The length of your list, the downright quantity, may threaten to undermine all your good intentions. Don't let it! If you must justify expenses, remember there is no mini-mart or all night Stop 'n' Shop on the third wave from the left. Once you have put out to sea, that's it, mate. You are provisioning for a totally self-contained unit, without replenishment possibilities, for quite a spell. That adds up to a heap of ship's stores.

Remember that mountain expedition I mentioned? Think of what they must have spent—all for naught, because the somebody doing *their* pre-planning lacked your preparation skills, discipline and plain good judgment. You're already ahead of the game, gal!

Yes, the COST OF IT ALL may seem horrendous, but again, do not cut your list back on quantity, once you have set up your menus and shopping list. Cut back instead by substituting margarine for butter, by using powdered eggs for all baking (stores easier and tastes nearly as good), by buying generic or house brands. But DO NOT let yourself be talked out of one single pound of that margarine, or a package of spaghetti or a can of tomato sauce...or a bottle of wine. Stick to your pre-planned quantity and variety, which you have just spent so much effort to determine, based on *your* knowledge of *your* crew's tastes and the sizes of their appetites.

...Once out to sea, however, you can be flexible with daily menu changes, if called for. If tonight's dinner needs to use up those foods which will spoil otherwise, go ahead. Food waste is not the name of the game, and you have already figured out the overall nutritional needs, so a switch here and there is no big deal.

...Remember the fishing gear...and the dill weed, white cooking wine and lemons to cook the catch in, and with!

...We have talked about night watch food and supplemental high energy food, which should provide all the sugar and triglycerides you need. But if there will be a birthday or an anniversary en route, add a package or two of cake mix to have for the big day, along with a can of frosting and the appropriate candles. Or try a package of fudge brownie mix to bake up and serve with instant chocolate pudding (dusted with shredded coconut and chocolate sprinkles.)

...Plan a surprise. What the hey—plan a *couple* of surprises: the half-way point celebration, a particularly sensational day of sailing, that wondrous star-filled night sail. For these special times, tuck in a bottle or two of champagne, ready-to-pop popcorn or extra-special dessert treats. Highlights such as these help make the adventure so much more special. And I guarantee, they won't be easily forgotten.

**9**

*CLEAN>>>>>*

*The Body…*

*…and the Bristol Craft*

**"After the first four years, the dirt doesn't get any worse."**                    *— Quentin Crisp*

*THE BODY...*

Think about it. The limited water supply, the lack of washing space for both body and the clothes that cover it. Kind of wows you?

Never fear, this too, is no big deal.

No one says you *have* to complete the whole job in fresh water. Fact is, you shouldn't. As long as the final *rinse* is fresh, the washing part can be done in salt water, recycled water from previous use, or rainwater you have collected. Another worthwhile rule of thumb: When you do get a supply of rainwater, reserve half for personal hygiene. The main challenge here is to avoid like the plague any salt sores. In fact, consider those as a plague of their own, especially around the bathing suit areas.

Rinse swimwear in a miniscule amount of your carefully collected rainwater, or no more than a cup of fresh, after each use. Apply this formula to rinsing underwear as well if you do laundry while underway: Wash in salt water to save your water supply, using a biodegradable detergent such as Joy®, but *always* rinse in fresh water or collected rainwater. You will only need a tiny bit and you'll avoid a lot of pain and agony.

> Recapping the rules of the road: Wash in heated salt water, rinse in fresh or rainwater, towel dry your body (do not let the salt water dry on you), and do not sit around in wet swim suits.

Hot water for showers can be had by investing in the plastic container sold at most chandleries which is filled with water and lashed on deck in the sun. Another trick is to buy a plastic garden sprayer, the kind landlubbers use to spray for garden pests. Paint it black to attract heat, fill with water and lash it on deck. Showering in the cockpit has to have the best view in town—for you. If you're at anchor, better drape the lifelines with towels or it could be the best one for everyone else, too!

Shampoo your hair in salt water; it's a great conditioner. No kidding. I know, you are thinking of your stiff streaked hair after swimming, but chlorine in the pool or not using shampoo with warm water were the real culprits. Heat the salt water, use either a regular shampoo or Joy®, and rinse in fresh or rain water. The results are great.

Body dirt is not the problem at sea that it is on land. For one thing, no smog. When you perspire, it is clean sweat; we found ourselves showering much less when cruising. But, just because you are at sea does not mean you can stop using deodorant or shaving your legs. Femininity is so necessary at times, right??

If the water you are sailing in can be swum in, you can clean in it, too. A washcloth or sponge, along with your dishwashing detergent, does wonders. Don't wrinkle your nose at the thought of washing your body with detergent. If it is bio-degradable, you will do ecology a favor, your hair will gleam, and all that salt crust, suntan oil and seawater collecting on your tender body will go away.

When bathing and performing personal hygiene in colder climates, choose the "bedbath" method: a small supply of water in a small container…and hurry!

As for toiletries, you will need pretty much what you use on land; e.g., deodorants, toothpaste and mouthwash. Just make sure the containers are plastic and are non-aerosol.

### ... AND THE BRISTOL CRAFT

If housework isn't your favorite challenge in life, you will love life at sea! But even small vessels require daily and occasional cleaning, just as any beloved home; and this vessel after all, is...or will be...your chosen home for a spell.

On a daily basis, you will find yourself still wiping down the stove and cooking areas, sprucing up the bathroom-in-this-case-the-head, washing and putting away dishes and cutlery, straightening the bunk cushions and sweeping up crumbs.

The weekly (or as needed) cleaning will include wiping down the portholes. If they are plastic, use warmed vinegar water; salt water scratches and the fresh water is too precious, unless of course you can catch some extra rainwater. Wipe down bulkheads with teak oil and a soft cloth, keep the stove from getting too grimy, clean and deodorize the ice chest, air all the bedding.

Most of this will take a sunny calm day and some baking soda. You can't store the sunny or the calm, but do put in a good supply of baking soda; it is versatile, inexpensive and ecological to boot. It can be used to extinguish a galley fire, clean the ice chest interior, food preparation surfaces and the stove. It helps get rid of coffee pot stains and cleans plastic of every kind. It helps you sweeten up the head, too, without resorting to harsh cleaners (not advisable, anyway).

In addition, this miracle worker helps in the first aid and personal hygiene departments: It deodorizes, it gives relief from sunburn and insect bites, it can be used as a tooth powder. Taken with warm water it becomes an antacid; as a cleaning aid, it helps get rid of any seasickness odor (ugh). If your dish towels are becoming less than socially acceptable, soak them in seawater and baking soda, then rinse. Great little invention, baking soda. Along with petroleum jelly and duck tape, it should get you just about anywhere you want to go.

For doing serious laundry between ports-of-call (where you can usually find a coin-wash establishment), you will have to rely on the old-fashioned bucket and washboard, topside. Again, choose a sunny calm day, use warm or hot salt water, rinse undies in a miniscule amount of fresh, dry in the sun either draped and secured to lifelines with wooden clothespins...even plastic ones have metal springs which will rust...or laid flat on the cabin. Things will get clean, and just think—no ironing afterwards!

**Here's David!**

*10*

*<<<<<AND HEALTHY*

*The Library*

*The Ship's Medicine Chest*
*Supplies—Medications*

*"God heals and the doctor takes the fee."*

— *Benjamin Franklin,* Poor Richard's Almanac

Remember back a bit, I allowed that several people had input into this book? The following was written by one David Stewart, our friend and chiropractor. David is a competent skipper in his own right, both as master of his own Ericson 32 *Lumbaygo* (first boat was *Slipped Disc*), and as a crew racer to Hawaii (serving as the ship's doctor), among other seafarin' expeditions. For Gene's singlehanded race to Hawaii, he voluntarily prepared and presented Gene with his shipboard first aid kit.

At my request, David listed the contents of that kit, made a few notes, and then gave me verbal permission to edit as I saw fit.

So here's David…almost verbatim.

\* \* \* \* \* \* \* \*

"This list of supplies and equipment is intended for a cruising vessel with a crew of two to six, embarking on a passage of two to six weeks away from shore help. While some basic first aid knowledge is helpful, a cool head in a crisis combined with a good library and medicine chest is far more important. Most health problems at sea can be controlled by a layman until port and professional help is reached.

**THE LIBRARY: *Three books no boat should be without***

**1) *ADVANCED FIRST AID AND EMERGENCY CARE***
American National Red Cross, 17th and D Street N.W., Wash, DC 20006;

**2) *THE SHIPS MEDICINE CHEST AND MEDICAL AID AT SEA***
HEW Publication No. (HSA) 78-2024, U.S. Government Printing Office

**3) *MERCK MANUAL***
Merck, Sharpe and Dohme, Rathway, NJ 07065

"All three of these volumes may be purchased at marine book stores, chandleries, or technical book stores.

"There are several other books available, most notably: *The Cruising Sailors Medical Guide* from David McCay Co., Inc., 2 Park Avenue, New York, NY 10016.

"For basic education in first aid, take a local CPR class (CPR: cardio pulmonary resuscitation). Your fire department or Red Cross office can direct you. The Red Cross basic first aid course is great training, and you need not get certified to learn."

### THE SHIP'S MEDICINE CHEST

#### *SUPPLIES (In No Special Order)*

- Tweezers, sharply pointed

- Razor blades, single-edged and/ or a scalpel handle and blades

- Safety pins, 2" — 1 dozen

- Airway, plastic

- Instant cold packs — Box of 6

- Boards for splints (can use existing boat pieces) or air splints, one for arm, one for leg

- Sling

- Tourniquet (this can be made up from cloth)

- Hot water bottle/ice bag with enema attachment

- Thermometer

- Pen light and extra batteries

- Tongue depressors, l dozen  (ask your doctor for these; they come from suppliers in huge quantities)

- Pliers, 8" needle-nosed with wire cutter built in

- Scissors, bandage-type (has one end blunted)

- Snake bite kit

- Cotton-tipped applicators such as Q-Tips®. The long wooden ones are best

- Ace® elastic bandages, 3" wide — Minimum of 2

- Bandage, sterile gauze roller, 3" x 10 yds. — Minimum of 3

- Bandage,  2" gauze squares — l box

- Bandage,  6" gauze squares — l box

- Adhesive tape,  2" rolls — 4 each

- Adhesive tape,  2" hypoallergenic, surgical — 4 each

- Dermicel© adhesives — 4 each

- Disinfectant soap

- Coconut oil soap (one that works in salt water)

- Cotton, sterile, absorbant — 1 box

### EXTRAS

- Suturing package with hemostat

- Sphygmomanometer and stethoscope

- Urinary catheter kit

## MEDICATIONS

Check with your family physician for specific needs, especially allergies. Many of the medications listed here are sold by prescription only, especially in the United States, so your family physician will be most helpful.

Items listed in [brackets] are alternatives to orthodox medications.

- Alka-Seltzer® [comfrey tea or 1 tablespoon of vinegar in a glass of water]

- Antiseptic: hydrogen peroxide, or Bactine® spray, or soap and water

- Burn ointment: Foille© [vitamin E oil or aloe vera gel]

*TIP: I have heard, too, that both meat tenderizer and papaya work for sunburns and jellyfish stings.*

*TIP: Keep at least one bottle of D.A.G.© on board for just about anything: Can be used as a gargle and it is excellent and instant relief from insect bites and/or stings—you name it. D.A.G. is an Irish Moss extract containing phenolated iodine with organic borates. I cannot recommend it highly enough; get it from your physician or chiropractor. Since it does contain iodine, however, use with caution in the South Seas or where coral reefs abound.*

- Toothache kit or oil of cloves

- Sunscreen. Get both your usual strength and a bottle or tube of the strongest as recommended by your doctor.

*TIP:* **IMPORTANT:** *Make sure whatever you get is* **waterproof***, such as Bullfrog©. You may have to go to a sporting goods store or chandlery for this.*

- Calamine lotion, large bottle

- Ben Gay® or equivalent, large tube

- Seasickness Medication:  Scopalamine patches seem to work best but do have side effects that some people cannot tolerate. These are worn behind the ear for a maximum of 3 days. Dramamine® or Bonine® are alternate choices. The quantity depends on your crew—if no one usually gets seasick, carry enough for the entire crew for 10 days in case of storm. If any crew member is easily seasick, carry sufficient amount for that person for the entire voyage plus your storm reserve.

*TIP: The patches are by prescription only.*

- Vitamin C, powder form, 1 pound

*TIP: Get this, and any other vitamins you plan to carry, directly from a pharmaceutical house rather than the local drug store. We use Bronson Pharmaceuticals, St. Louis MO 63146. What you get will be pure goods without a lot of sugar and/or starch fillers, and at the most cost-efficient level.*

- Boric acid solution, 4 oz. bottle [chamomile tea]

- NoDoz® or equivalent for those long night watches

- Petroleum jelly, large jar

- Camphor ice for sunburned lips and cold sores. Cold sores can be miserable in a salt environment. 500 mg of L-Lysine (an amino acid from the health food store) taken daily is a preventive.

- Laxative. Your usual but also carry a stool softener for chronic constipation

- Kaopectate® or Imodium A-D® to combat diarrhea

- Metamucil®

- Milk of magnesia

- Lomotil

*TIP: This is for the* **severe** *diarrhea sometimes referred to as "The Green Apple Two Step." Suggest you get the kind without the antibiotics added. Prescription needed in U.S.A. but not below the U.S./ Mexican border.*

- Rubbing alcohol — 1 bottle

- "Smelling salts" — Aromatic ammonia inhalant, crushable ampules

- A broad spectrum antibiotic such as Ampicillin capsules — 250 mg bottle

- Aspirin or equivalent — 1 large bottle

- Codeine sulfate 30 mg tablets — 1 bottle

- Morphine sulfate injection. This is a narcotic to be used only for heavy duty pain.

- Hemorrhoidal suppositories

- Ipecac syrup

- Penicillin or other oral antibiotic tablets

- Quinine sulfate tables (if you will be in a malarial area)

- Salt tablets

- Tetracycline hydrochloride capsules

.* * * * * * * *

Thanks again, David. You are the ***greatest!***

The list looks endless and ominous, but these supplies take up surprisingly little space. Choose the driest spot for storage, but make sure it is immediately accessible. A small hammock strung amidships over the V-berth (away from hatchway drips) is a good idea: won't spill, stays dry and the supplies are reasonably handy when needed. Or again, the bottom of your hanging locker.

One additional tip: Separate the medications according to treatment needed (e.g., seasickness, constipation, "Green Apple Two-Step," colds, sunburns). Bag each group in double Ziplocs® and label the treatment group *clearly*. Saves time when put to use, believe me.

NOTE: For those of you who wear contact lenses, we suggest you not only carry along extra quantity of the cleansing solution, but ***take special heed of this caution:*** In saltwater surroundings, ***it is strongly advised that you clean your contact lenses at least once a day.*** Salt can build up on top of the lenses themselves, but worse, can build up between the lens and your eyeball. With the eyeball moving for visual impacts, this movement against the lens, along with the insertion of salt water, creates a sandpaper effect. At best, you will have a scratched eyeball; at worst, the eyes are severely damaged if not recognized soon enough.

Your sight is too important to take any chances. Consider keeping your contact lenses for land and wearing regular glasses while at sea.

*Are We Having Fun Yet?*

# *11*

*ENUFF ALREADY!!*

**"Be tolerant of the skipper who disagrees with you; he has a right
to his ridiculous opinions!"**

Nobody expects you to be a smiling Pollyanna every damn day. You can be the best First Mate in the world, but if the weather has been downright putrid for days on end…if the rockin' and rollin' and pitching just *will not stop*, even you, sainted one, can have an off day.

When that day comes, maybe the following will help restore your balance.

### *TEN (TONGUE-IN-CHEEK) WAYS TO BE A FIRST RATE FIRST MATE*

*1.* *STAY HEALTHY.* Under no circumstances must you catch a cold, get a toothache or contract the monthlies. Without even considering the sheer havoc the implements of the latter can do to marine plumbing, any one of these weaknesses will undermine all that propaganda of A Healthy Life At Sea; the same propaganda that *right this minute* some scheming skipper is selling as a bill of goods to some unsuspecting spouse or lover.

Above all, if the boat is breaking up under you, for God's sake **DO NOT** get in the way. You might end up with a broken bone or something and that just upsets The Captain.

There *is* one exception. You can get seasick if you want; just make sure it's over in time to fix dinner.

2. ***BE CREATIVE IN THE GALLEY.*** With a little imagination and a lot of mayo, you can create a full-blown dinner out of a can of sauerkraut and some moldy lunch meat. Well, if not full-blown, at least a tasty casserole. Just cover the whole thing with crushed potato chips and bake. If you are already out of potato chips…frankly, I don't know what you're going to do.

3. ***SERVE THE MEAL WITH FLAIR.*** Now, I cannot really recommend candlelight. We all know if the wind and waves didn't roar up just as you started to cook, it's a sure bet they will when you get ready to serve. The resulting water through the hatch that puts out the stove will also get the candle. Look at it this way, though: all that water is handy to clean up the mess.

   Choose a pretty tablecloth, but do refrain from grabbing the bright red sailbag so handy in the forepeak. Chances are, too, that the sail is still in the bag and this makes for a lumpy table. Chances are also—this is sure to be the next sail The Captain needs. Finding it on the table will *really* upset him.

   By the way, you *can* actually serve dinner *in* the oven, given the right set of circumstances (such as the result of The Captain and the boat playing with sail configurations again). This method saves washing dishes as the food is served directly from the oven walls. All you need are the utensils to scrape everything up, and the oven door is such a cozy table for two, as the food is served warm and steaming: warm food, steaming First Mate.

4. ***DARE TO BE DIFFERENT.*** One way to avoid the collision of food and cabin sole is to time all meals for calm waters only. Lunch: 3:00 am, every other Tuesday??

5. ***DEVELOP A TOUGH SKIN.*** Literally. Or barring that, flameproof gloves come in handy when transferring the boiling water from pot to cups—they help deaden the pain. Also, should you develop black and blue marks on your hips and thighs from constantly being tossed into the stove knobs, keep these colors in mind when selecting next summer's swimwear. A polka dot pattern would be nice.

6.  ***FORGET FEMININE TRAITS.*** What with all the bulky sweatshirts and foul weather gear, there's not a whole lot of outside evidence anyways. Primarily what this means is, ***do not cry*** when The Captain screams from the foredeck "Pull up on the halyard, godamnit!" and you —already pulling for all your worth, of course— yell back "***I am*** pulling, you Son of A Sea Cook!" Here, a teary trembly voice just doesn't cut it.

    While we are on the subject of yelling, every First Mate needs one of those tee shirts that loudly proclaim **DON'T SHOUT AT ME!** Not that it will do a damn bit of good (whoever heard of a Skipper or Captain who didn't shout?), but you WILL have gone on record that—though you sure as hell can hear him, and will defend to the death his right to give orders on his very own boat—you do not think much of his form of delivery.

7.  ***BE NEAT.*** There Is No Room On A Boat For Clutter. A Place For Everything And Everything In Its Place. Tartly repeat these necessary homilies to your Captain if he should get upset just because you hung up his foul weather gear as he was shedding it. The fact that you are sailing through a monsoon and all he wants is a quick dry dinner has nothing to do with it.

8.  ***BE COMPANIONABLE.*** Well, sometimes. Now I am sure your Skipper is just dying to hear all about the latest happenings and breakdowns in the galley. It's just that his interest has a tendency to ebb when he is in the middle of honing in on a difficult sextant shot from a rolling deck. Besides, he thinks you're manning the chronometer.

    It is also tough to get his attention when he is concentrating on tedious mathematics while plotting the results of that fix. Oh, you will get his attention all right…that's not the problem. It will be robust, vocal and awfully noisy, **that's** the problem. If you have small children on board, now is a good time to send them out to play.

9.   **BE CONTROLLED.**  To be specific, learn to control interior female plumbing to a SlowMo, such as three times a week. While the good male Captain always has his lee rail, you are stuck with the head and naturally, the boat is on the wrong tack to pump. It always is.

Speaking of the lee rail, I once heard a little girl, observing a little boy, comment "My, that's certainly a handy gadget to take along on a picnic!" Where is some enterprising inventor to invent an adapter for female First Mates that really works? Just think of it: With a little mass market know-how, there could be adapter gadgets in every chandlery in the land. Maybe the supermarkets would pick it up…feature it, even: right between the peanut butter and the pickles.

Or how about foul weather gear with scads of Velcro©? The Captain gets Velcro, why can't female First Mates get Velcro? Discrimination, that's what it is.

10.   **BE OPEN-MINDED.** If in the middle of all this spilling, yelling and lee railing, your stalwart Captain looks you straight in the eye and in That Voice murmurs "I'm so proud of you, I don't know HOW you manage. God, I love you!"…well, you have one of two choices: Tell him to stuff it, stow it, and sit on it; or…discount all of the above, give him a resounding kiss that promises a whole lot more if this damn boat will every settle down, breathe deeply and carry on, knowing you adore this sailing life just as much as he does, even with a bum day now and then.

Frankly, I recommend the latter!

*On the High Seas—This IS Where It's At!*

## *12*

*RANDOM THOUGHTS: A FINAL POTPOURRI*

*Suggested Reading Supplements*

*Long Distance Communication with Home*

*Finances*

*Nothing in Particular and Everything Worthwhile*

*"I only ask to be free. The butterflies are free."*                    *— Charles Dickens*

### *SUGGESTED READING SUPPLEMENTS*

Along with the medical books suggested in Chapter 10, there are four general books which, in our humble opinion, no vessel should be without. We consider these the "sailing bibles" for references:

***SAIL POWER,*** by Wallace Ross with Carl Chapman, published by Alfred A. Knopf, New York. Without a doubt, the answer to any question you might have regarding sails lies between its covers.

***THE OCEAN SAILING YACHT,*** by Donald Street, published by W. W. Norton and Company, Inc., New York.

***FROM A BARE HULL,*** by Ferenc Matè, published by Albatross Publishing of Vancouver, BC.

These latter two books cover just about any topic of sailing, cruising, boat construction—you name it.

In addition, get and keep aboard a copy of ***PILOTING SEASMANSHIP AND SMALL BOAT HANDLING,*** by Charles F. Chapman, published by Motor Boating, New York, NY. This one is a veritable tome, but a necessary one. Gives all details on equipment and lights, rules of the road, compassing, aids to navigation, charts and piloting, and much more as well.

The copyright details are dated on all of these books, but the information gleaned is timeless.

Speaking of books, please!—do ***not*** remove any to save weight. In fact, get more: paperbacks, of course, of ***any and all subject matter.*** You won't be sorry, and neither will your crew. Even people who normally don't read a lot will read on a boat—and sometimes quite a bit.

## LONG DISTANCE COMMUNICATION WITH HOME

D o you plan to? Keep in touch, I mean. Do you want friends, family and land-locked acquaintances to reach you while you are en route? If so, advance preparation will be required.

The logical mail drop would be yacht clubs and/or marinas. However, many of them have rather short seasons that are crammed full, so the possibility is always there that your messages or mail could get lost. Post offices in the towns or villages you plan to visit will hold mail addressed to you in care of General Delivery, but what if you decide at the last minute to forego that particular stop?

There is no cut and dried solution; my best suggestion would be for **YOU** to be the Communicat**OR** to all your Communicat**EES**. Leave as detailed an itinerary as possible with someone at home, including the phone numbers for yacht clubs or marinas that you *know* you will be visiting.

Other than that, you *are* out of touch with the home front. Isn't that the whole idea???

## *FINANCES*

T he same "vacation" rule applies to long-range cruising that applies elsewhere: namely, whatever you think it will take, take more. In out-of-the-way ports of call, food, supplies and a drink at the local bar might cost more than you think.

Take both cash and travelers checks (stored in the driest part of the boat, and in double-bagged Ziplocs© of course). It is best not to rely on major credit cards or personal checks for every contingency, but since major problems can arise—should you need to write a check for a major boat repair job or a medical emergency, for instance—take the time and precaution *now* to let your local bank official know what you are about. You are then covered should the need arise, as this action will give them the authorization to verify your bank balance or provide a personal description, if necessary.

Verify your line of credit on your major credit card. If you feel it could or should be greater, get it increased now.

If yours is to be a lengthy sojourn at sea, give some thought to the bills that come in monthly and would pile up in your absence. They go unpaid and your credit rating takes a nosedive. Appoint someone trustworthy as your "treasurer," give them a supply of signed checks and let them pay your bills as they come in, or add them to the list of authorized signatures on your account. This, of course, will entail that same somebody making deposits to your checking account, or being in charge of it. The whole subject is worth its own discussion and careful, thoughtful preplanning.

## *NOTHING IN PARTICULAR AND EVRYTHING WORTHWHILE*

…Schedule yourself for the 0300-0600 watch. Have you ever witnessed the shooting stars that seem to be visible in the clarity of the night skies found only at sea? Or seen the world come awake as you watch the emerging glorious sunrise painted for your benefit alone, while standing at the helm of your vessel on a shimmering morning sea—and somebody else hands *you* the first mug of steaming coffee??

While on that watch, look and listen for the gentle and gracious dolphins who seem to come from nowhere, sailing in tempo with your vessel; will they brush your elbow… as they did mine…with their graceful leaps as you sit on the port helm? They love to surf through the glowing and mystical phosphorescence, a result of plankton in the sea, that is reflected in your vessel's running lights.

A wondrous sight indeed! And listen! YES! They *do* seem to call out: "Come race with us, pretty boat!"

Yep. This *is* what it's all about. As they say, "It don't get any better'n this!"

"No life worth living is totally free from chance, but we feel
less danger, more in accord with the one God of our choice
in a boat of our choice, on a one-to-one basis with the sea and
the elements and each other. Better, we feel, than freeways
and intersections jammed with the nuts who just had a fight
with spouse or boss, the nuts spaced out on God-knows-what,
roaring down behind the wheel of a car…and we're the
next one encountered.

Nope. One to one. The odds are better."

*…D.H., Almosts Only Count In Horseshoes and Play For More.*

*Happy sailing with fair winds always, Mate!*

# Appendices A to E

## WHAT DO THEY COVER?

### APPENDIX A:
*Menus Tried and True: Hawaii Race*

### APPENDIX B:
*Recipes In Two Parts*

### APPENDIX C:
*Food/Supply Inventory Lists*

### APPENDIX D:
*Floor Plans*

### APPENDIX E:
*Suggestions and Tips from the Captain*

# *Appendices*

## *WHAT DO THEY COVER?*

### *APPENDIX A—MENUS TRIED AND TRUE*

These are for reference to be used either as a jumping-off place or verbatim. Remember I mentioned that all-male-crewed race that Gene skippered to Hawaii? This is what they ate.

Since this particular vessel had a freezer and a microwave and I did a fair amount of pre-cooking and freezing, I have occasionally referenced using both these appliances. If there is no freezer on your vessel—and with reference to those dishes listed as stored in the freezer—you will have to rely on canned meats (for the stroganoff perhaps) and ready-made containers (spaghetti sauce with meat, cans of split pea soup, etc.). Some breads will have to be baked as you cruise. Don't panic: It's easy and…honest, fun to do!

See the end of Appendix A for further pre-cook/freeze substitution suggestions, as well as additional menu item ideas requiring minimal refrigeration capability.

Note that these menus also give both food locale and instructions for the meal preparation. These made up Part 1 of Section 1 in that now infamous 3-ring binder mentioned in Chapter 8. Part 2 of the first section in that notebook were the actual recipes for those items duly referenced in the menu section. I list all this here, although the comments and directions given for preparation may seem sophomoric, but remember: It was an all-male crew, none of whom were super savvy in the galley. I didn't want to take any chances!

You will also note the on-going reference to the word "Bag" with either a B, L, or D, and a number. These refer to Breakfast, Lunch, Dinner, Day 1, Day 5, Day 10, etc. I tried to consolidate the whole meal into individual bags for easy retrieval; the bag also contained the directions to find and cook any perishables and items not included in the bags.

Talk about covering all the bases…these guys had no excuses.

## APPENDIX B—RECIPES, IN TWO PARTS

✳ Part 1 is the first section in the go-along notebook. Here are those recipes (designated by the symbol shown here) from the actual race menus. Pretty basic, mate; you probably won't need them.

Part 2 offers a few more, included here for thought and good measure.

## APPENDIX C—FOOD/SUPPLY INVENTORY LISTS:
### 1) Location; 2) Alphabetically by Item

Sections 3 and 4 of the notebook, respectively. These are the actual inventory lists I made out for the Hawaiian race. This also includes the packing list for the freezer, the item and what meal and day it is for.

The above is offered with the fervent hope it all helps to get you started.

## APPENDIX D—Floor Plans

For thought and review and possible application, here are the vessel layouts from both our vessel and the 53' ketch, diagramming how space was delegated to food and supply—storage and stowage (storage: for retrieval at a later date; stowage: securing safely).

"Whither Thou" is not exactly at the bottom of the list for a well-outfitted vessel but she does lack—by choice—a refrigeration system, a water pressure system, has no microwave or freezer, and no one can open a door and walk into HER engine room (except maybe an agile Munchkin!) The 53' ketch had all this, although she was not at the top of the list, either.

So the spectrum is fairly wide. No doubt your vessel lies somewhere in and around. Apply information where needed and discuss, discard or utilize as best for you.

## APPENDIX E—SUGGESTIONS AND TIPS FROM THE CAPTAIN

Off-the-cuff suggestions and tips from Gene directed to both the Captain and crew. These are based on his previously published articles and deal with such subject matter as jury-rigging and alternate sail configuration considerations.

The menus for the first few days took into consideration the possibility of seasickness on board and/or seas too rough for extensive meal preparation. Use those shown below for Days 1 to 4 as coastal supplements to the suggestions given in the subhead in Chapter 8, "The First Bumpy Days."

Directions for *meal preparation* are in italics.

✳ This symbol denotes that directions for preparation for the crew are under "Recipes." For you, mate, see Appendix B.

You'll note here and there a *"TIP."* These are also directed to you, First Mate, not the Hawaii-bound crew. Okay! Here we go!

| DAY/MEAL/COMMENTS | MENU  ITEM(S) and DIRECTIONS |
|---|---|
| **DAY #1 (include date/day of the week if you wish)** | |
| *Breakfast* | *Will be served prior to departure.* |
| *Lunch* | To be fruit only, bananas and/or pears |
| *Dinner* | Instant noodle mug soup (l each) |
| | French Bread (top of freezer) |
| | Instant individual-sized pudding cans |
| | *"D-1" Bag (either in #3 or in the sink) holds everything but the bread.* |
| | *Remove bread from foil if using microwave to heat; put on a paper plate. Leave in foil if using regular oven.* |

**"A good cook is like a sorceress who dispenses happiness."**                    **— Esa Schiaparelli**

| | |
|---|---|
| *NIGHT WATCH SNACKS* | All in #5B. These do not include coffee, tea bags or honey. Strongly suggest avoiding coffee at night; substitute hot cocoa or hot tea liberally laced with honey (galley D). |

*DAY #2*

**Breakfast**

✳ Orange juice. *Use quart pitcher (yellow) for all fruit juices.*

Melon slices (in hammock), choice of instant hot oatmeal or cold cereal, with milk

Coffee—tea—hot cocoa (Nestlè Quik© using milk, or Carnation© using hot water)

**NOTE: Coffee, tea, cocoa to be available at every meal. Will not be listed hereafter.**

*Hot oatmeal or cold cereals: Bag "B-2," Locker #2. Use other quart pitcher (white) to mix dry milk and water.*

*Cut one melon into individual servings.*

**Lunch**

Instant soup mugs without noodles

Apple, cheese wedges

Instant soup mug containers in Bag "L-2," Locker #2 Apples in bag and in hammock, cheese in lower frig

**Dinner**

Instant noodle mug soup mix (2 servings each)

French bread

Salad (optional)

Individual puddings, ready to eat

*Soup and puddings in Bag "D-2," Locker #2*

*Bread in freezer, marked "D-2"*

*Heat bread (see "D-1" suggestion). Make salad using lettuce, 2 or 3 tomatoes, zucchini, bottled dressing or oil and vinegar (galley H). Salt and pepper to taste. Use lettuce as directed please, and leave the cabbage for later!*

## DAY #3

**Breakfast**

Instant hot cereals or individual cold cereal packages with sliced bananas (in hammock)

✳ Orange juice (Tang© Orange mix and Wylers© lemonade mix)

Toasted english muffins

*Toast if using the generator. Otherwise butter and brown in the frying pan. Muffins in lower frig marked "B-3"*

**Lunch**

Packaged instant soups (not the mug with noodles)

Saltine crackers

*Both in Bag "L-3"*

Cheese

Apples or bananas (in hammock), cheese in frig.

*Use any or all varieties of bulk cheeses and sliced luncheon meat if desired. Do not use sliced American cheese: that is for a later menu.*

| | |
|---|---|
| ***Dinner*** | Baked potatoes with browned meat and gravy |

Salad

Cheesecake and canned pears

*Gravy mix, cheese cake mix and fruit are in Bag "D-3"
Potatoes in hammock, meat is in "D-3" in freezer*

*Defrost meat (all day at room temp or about 20 min in
microwave)*

*Sauté (brown) meat (with a sliced onion if desired) in
fry pan. Prepare gravy mix per directions on package.
Combine gravy and meat, serve over hot split potatoes.*

*Make salad using 2nd head of lettuce, 2 or 3 tomatoes,
green pepper, green onions, zucchini. Serve with oil and
vinegar or a bottled dressing.*

*Follow directions for cheese cake (use powdered milk).
Serve with warmed pear halves.*

*Milk in galley C*

**PUT V-8© JUICE IN FRIG FOR TOMORROW
MORNING. LOCATED IN #1.**

***DAY #4***

***Breakfast***    1 grapefruit half each (in hammock or aft shower)

Hot coffee cake

Hot or cold cereals. *Serve with warmed canned peach
slices* (In galley C)

V-8© juice (in frig or #1)

2 coffee cake mixes and hot cereals in Bag "B-4."
Follow directions on package for coffee cake (bake
both). Add $\frac{1}{2}$ cup chopped raisins to each pan, sprinkle
both with nut topping.

**Lunch**

Grilled cheese sandwiches on whole wheat bread—
1 or 2 per person

Fresh fruit (apples or oranges)

Soup if desired

*Use the sliced American individually-wrapped cheese,
located in frig. Bread in freezer marked "L-4," two
containers. Fruit(s) in hammock, soup in Bag "L-4."*

*Soup preparation per package directions. Butter out-
side of bread and put 2 slices cheese per sandwich
between slices. Brown in fry pan and serve immediately.*

*Makings are for 2 sandwiches per person. If more
desired, cheese slices are in frig. Refrigerate or re-
freeze unused bread, re-wrap in foil.*

**Dinner**

Beer Stew

Bisquick© biscuits or leftover french bread, if any

Salad

Brownies and chocolate pudding

Bisquick©, brownies and pudding in Bag "D-4"

✳ (For biscuits) *Defrost stew (in freezer marked "D-
4") and heat thoroughly. Heat bread in foil or make
biscuits.*

*Make salad with 3rd head of lettuce and any remaining fresh ingredients. If desired, make fresh salad dressing (see mixes in locker #5). Otherwise, use bottled or oil and vinegar.*

*If desired, prepare brownies per directions and serve after dishes are done, with or without pudding. Pudding directions on box; use freshly made milk if possible.*

**GET GRAPEFRUIT JUICE FROM #1 AND PUT IN FRIG FOR MORNING.**

**DAY #5**

**Breakfast**

Grapefruit juice, 2 eggs any style, canned bacon

Toasted english muffins with jam or honey

*Juice in frig or #1, bacon in #2, eggs in frig under shelf (if none on shelf), muffins lower frig marked "B-5," jam and honey galley D*

*Wash bacon thoroughly to remove excess salt. Caution to everyone: Go easy on adding salt to eggs and bacon…this canned stuff is potent!*

*Butter and brown muffins in fry pan, then put in oven to keep warm while frying bacon and fixing the eggs.*

**Lunch**

Leftover stew or instant soup mix

✳ Bisquick© biscuits

Apple and cheese wedges

*Instant soup mix containers and biscuit mix in "L-5." Apples in hammock. Cheese and stew (if any) in frig*

*If having stew, heat thoroughly. Make biscuits per directions under "Recipes."*

**Dinner**              Split pea soup, french bread, cabbage salad

Fresh pudding and cookies

*Soup in freezer marked "D-5." Salad ingredients (nuts, vegetables, bacon dressing), pudding and cookies in Bag "D-5."*

*Defrost soup and heat thoroughly over low heat; oven-heat last of french bread (in freezer D-5), make as garlic bread if desired (mix oleomargarine and garlic powder, spread on each slice prior to heating in foil).*

*Cut or shred half a head of green cabbage, and a quarter head of red. Combine with toasted sunflower seeds, croutons (both in galley H) and well-drained jar of mixed-bean-salad vegetables (#1). Toss with freshly made bacon dressing (oil and vinegar galley H).*

*Make puddings and cookies per directions on boxes, but only if desired. You guys don't need all these sweets.*

**NOTE: If soup is too thin, thicken with flour/milk paste.**

*DAY #6*

**Breakfast**         ☀  Hot cakes

☀  Orange Juice

Melon wedges

*Pancake mix in galley B. See "Recipes." Mix juice per directions in "Recipes." Cut 2nd melon into equal servings. Syrup, galley H. Jam in galley D or frig.*

|  |  |
|---|---|
| ***Lunch*** | Leftover pea soup (if none left, use the Top Ramen©) |
|  | Crackers, cheese wedges and lunch meat slabs |
|  | Packaged soup and crackers in Bag "L-6." Cheese, lunch meat in frig. More crackers in either galley D or #4 |
|  | If using Top Ramen©, and if desired, add chopped onion and any remaining fresh salad ingredients to soup (green pepper, etc.). See directions on package. |
| ***Dinner*** | Tossed salad |
|  | Spaghetti with Parmesan cheese |
|  | ✳ Beer Bread |
|  | Cheesecake |
|  | *Spaghetti sauce in freezer marked "D-6," Parmesan cheese in frig or #5, cheesecake #5A, spaghetti noodles in #4* |
|  | *Make beer bread per "Recipes"; only takes 45 minutes total. Cook noodles (use at least 1 full 12 oz. package of for all of you—may need more).* |
|  | *Defrost and heat the sauce. Serve over noodles, top with cheese. Make lettuce salad using last of the lettuce.* |
|  | *If desired, make cheesecake and serve 1 to 2 hours after dinner.* |

*DAY #7*

|  |  |
|---|---|
| ***Breakfast*** | Grapefruit half (aft shower) and orange juice |
|  | 2 eggs, any style (suggest poached or fried) with hash |

Bran muffins

*Canned hash in #1. Follow directions on cans, use 3 or 4.*

*Muffin mix in #5. Use enough packages to give 2 per person.*

**Lunch**          Macaroni and cheese

Apples and/or oranges, crackers

Crackers and macaroni and cheese (2 boxes) in Bag "L-7." Follow directions on boxes, use both.

**Dinner**         Cabbage salad

✳ Beef Stroganoff over chinese fried rice

Mixed vegetables

✳ Bisquick© biscuits

*The fried rice takes less than a half hour to prepare. Do it while the biscuits are in the oven, but cook the rice earlier. See "Recipes."*

*Stroganoff in freezer marked "D-7." Defrost and heat thoroughly. Before serving add a big spoon of: 1) sour cream and 2) a touch of Kitchen Bouquet© to darken. Thicken if necessary with a medium-thick paste made of 3) Wondra© flour and water blended in measuring cup.*

*1) Either fresh in frig or make one of the sour cream mixes, locker #5*

*2) and 3) In with spices, Galley G*

*Make cabbage salad using both green and red (approx. half a head of each), croutons, toasted nuts. Chef's choice of dressing.*

*Mixed vegetables (canned) in #1. May need to use both cans. Heat and serve with melted butter.*

*Spoon stroganoff over rice and serve.*

*If dessert desired, make up a pudding or a snacking cake.*

**TAKE OUT A CAN OF APPLE JUICE  (#1)  AND PUT IN FRIG FOR MORNING.**

*DAY #8*

**Breakfast**    ✳ Beer pancakes with warm sliced peaches (#1), syrup (galley  H) and powdered sugar (#5)

Apple juice (in frig or #1)

*NOTE: Hard-boil 6 eggs for lunch.*

**Lunch**    Egg salad sandwiches, 1 or 2 each

Apples (hammock) and potato chips (Locker #4)

*Bread (whole wheat) in freezer (L-8)*

*Mixed chopped eggs with chopped pickles (galley H), mayo (frig or #2). Chips in #4*

**Dinner**    Baked ham with applesauce (both in #2)

Mashed potatoes, instant (galley B)

Pork gravy (gravy mixes, #5)

Canned whole corn (# l. Use 2 cans)

Brownies, #5A

*Note: Keep out enough ham for breakfast on day #10, 1 slice each, medium thick).*

*Open ham, heat in low oven for about a half hour or so until heated through (cover with foil during this first heating). Spread with mixture of half mustard (in frig) and half honey (galley D); make about ³⁄₄ cup. Score top and put 1 whole clove (galley G) in each square or diamond. Continue heating, uncovered, until hot throughout.*

*Make mashed potatoes per instructions on container.*

*Gravy mix per instructions.*

*Heat 2 cans corn, drain and serve topped with butter.*

*Serve applesauce as meat accompaniment.*

*Make brownies if you must  - or -*

*It's been one whole week, gang. Treat yourself to popcorn.*

**TAKE PINEAPPLE JUICE OUT OF #1 AND PUT IN FRIG FOR MORNING.**

*DAY #9*

    *Breakfast*      Pineapple Juice (frig or #1), melon

                    ✳ Cereal, hot or cold, with raisins (galley C)

    *Lunch*         Top Ramen© soup #4, Crackers #4 or galley D

                     Cheese, lunch meat and apples

    *Dinner*       Baked chicken halves (in freezer, marked "D-9"; two bags, half a chicken per person). Cranberry sauce # 1, use 2 cans. Stuffing # 4, marked "D-9." Cabbage salad. Bisquick© biscuits (optional, and per previous instructions)

_Defrost and heat chicken halves thoroughly. Prepare stuffing per directions on box, make cabbage salad, chef's choice for dressing and ingredients._

_Pudding for dessert if desired._

**DAY #10**

**Breakfast**    Orange juice

Fried ham (in frig), 2 eggs (any style) (in frig)

Sliced pineapple #l. _May need both cans_

English muffins, toasted;  lower frig, "B-10"

**Lunch**    Ramen soup  #4

Crackers, cheese wedges, lunch meat slabs, apples

**Dinner**    Stew in freezer, "D-10"

Cabbage salad as usual

Biscuits

Cheesecake, if wanted, #5A

_Defrost stew, heat thoroughly. Prepare biscuits and salad. Chef's choices again. What is left??_

**_REMOVE TOMATO JUICE FROM #1 TO FRIG FOR MORNING._**

**DAY #11**

**Breakfast**    Coffee cake (#4) with warmed fruit cocktail (#1)

Hot or cold cereals, galley C

Tomato juice with Worcestershire sauce and celery salt (juice in frig or #1 spices in galley G)

*Bake coffee cake as before; use 2 packages. See day #4 for directions.*

**Lunch**          Grilled cheese sandwiches, 1 or 2 each

Apples, potato chips #4

*Use english muffins (4 packages), located in lower frig and marked "L-11). See day #4 lunch for directions. Cheese slices in frig.*

**Dinner**         Spaghetti, bread sticks, salad

*Sauce and noodles in #4. Bread sticks in freezer "D-11," heat sauce, cook noodles. serve with Parmesan cheese. salad is chef choice.*

Popcorn anyone?

**DAY #12**

**Breakfast**      Orange juice, 2 eggs, any style, canned bacon, bran muffins

See day #5/Breakfast for bacon hints. Muffins in #5. Follow directions.

**Lunch**          Tuna sandwiches, 1 or 2 each. Serve w/sliced pickles (galley H), apples, chips (Locker # 4)

*Bread in freezer, tuna fish in #1. Mix tuna, mayo, pickle relish (frig or #2)*

| | |
|---|---|
| ***Dinner*** | Chinese dinner, Locker #3 marked "D-12" |

Cabbage salad, Fortune cookies #3, Bag marked "D-12"

Snacking cake, locker #5A

*Use all cans of chinese dinner, prepare as directed on cans. Heat bean sprouts in sauce pan, heat noodles in oven. Chef choice on salad, suggest using shoestring beets, locker #1.*

**TAKE OUT APPLE JUICE FROM #1 AND PUT IN FRIG FOR MORNING.**

*TIP: When I joined the crew in Hawaii, they said this was the only thumbs-down dinner. I include it here only as it **was** part of the pre-planning, and how did I know most of them were oriental food connoisseurs?? Canned indeed...oh well, can't win 'em all. Still, it is a change of pace.*

***DAY #13***

    ***Breakfast***          Apple juice

✳ Hot cakes. See Days #6 and #8 breakfasts for serving hints

Warm peaches or fruit cocktail #1

    ***Lunch***          Top Ramen© Soup #4   Crackers  galley D or #4

Cheese and lunch meat wedges

**Dinner**                   Baked chicken. Freezer, "D-l3" with cranberry sauce #l. Use 2 cans.

Au gratin potatoes #4. Use it and the small box of scalloped potatoes as well, if desired

Canned peas with hollandaise sauce #1 and #5 respectively

Chocolate pudding and cookies.

*Defrost chicken; heat. Prepare potatoes per instructions on box. Heat peas; make sauce per directions on package. If desired, bake cookies and make pudding as directed on packages.*

**DAY #14**

**Breakfast**               Orange juice, 2 eggs any style, fried ham (#2)

Toasted muffins with jam or honey

*Open 2nd canned ham and slice half for breakfast.* **Keep other half for tomorrow's lunch.**

*Muffins in lower frig B-l4. Jams, etc., in galley D*

**Lunch**                   Pork 'n' Beans # l. Use 2 cans

Canned brown bread with cream cheese #2. Use 2 cans. Cheese in frig

Cheese wedges and apples, optional

*Heat beans with brown sugar, mustard and molasses.*

*Heat bread in oven; see direction on cans.*

|  |  |  |
|---|---|---|
| ***Dinner*** | ✳ Clams and linguine | Both in Bag "D-14" |

Salad (chef's choice)

✳ Beer Bread

Dessert/chef's choice. See #5A. **What is left, guys**?

Cook linguine same as spaghetti. See "Recipes" for rest of directions.

## DAY #15

***Breakfast***   Everything is chef's choice. What's left? Juices, canned fruits (warmed) with cereals, hot or cold.

***Lunch***   Ham and cheese sandwiches, 1 or 2 each (*use muffins in freezer*)

Fruit, canned or fresh (if any left)

***Dinner***   Baked potatoes with hamburger meat and chef's choice of gravy mix

Cabbage salad

*See day #3/Dinner for preparation. Meat in Freezer D-15.*

## SUBSTITUTION SUGGESTIONS
### *for PRE-COOKED and FROZEN MENU ITEMS*

**STEW**

Used the canned variety, but as suggested in Chapter 8 (Shopping List subhead), supplement the contents with additional herbs, onion, etc.

P. S."Beer" Stew is simply replacing part of the usual liquid with a can of fresh beer. Adds tart and taste but the alcohol cooks off.

**BEEF STROGANOFF**

Sauté fresh onion and canned mushrooms; use canned roast beef, sour cream package mix; heat bullion for the liquid. Thicken with flour-and-water paste darkened with a bit of Kitchen Bouquet©. Serve over rice or pasta.

**SPLIT PEA SOUP**
(or hearty main-dish type soup)

Use the top-quality canned variety (usually the price will clue you in) or get the dry package mixes and make from scratch with powdered milk. There are excellent pea, minestrone, and vegetable canned soups on the market, as well as chowders and bisques. For early on in the cruise, try the "soup starters" variety and add fresh ingredients.

When it comes to fish chowders, pre-cooked and then frozen is a real "iffy" from a health standpoint. I ended up burying a whole soup pot full of freshly made and laboriously fussed over clam chowder because it had inadvertently been left on top of the still-warm stove all night. Even though you might not do such a dumb thing, anything involving fresh fish and milk bases should be avoided as bacteria grows <u>so</u> fast in these host environments. Better to get the canned variety, prepare and embellish en route, or see Appendix B for the Clam Chowder recipe.

## *ADDITIONAL MENU/ITEM IDEAS REQUIRING*
## *MINIMUM OR NO REFRIGERATION*

| | |
|---|---|
| *TUNA FISH* | <u>CASSEROLE</u>: Get the water-packed variety, combine with noodles and a cream soup for a dinner menu;  or |
| | <u>WITH MACARONI</u>: Combine equal portions of tuna fish and packaged macaroni and cheese (1 can = 1package), add a can of mixed veggies or peas. Prepare macaroni per the package directions then add everything else. That's all, folks! Or, add a can of mushroom soup and a diced onion for added taste. |
| | <u>SALAD</u>: Mix with cooked salad macaroni, mayo, a bit of ketchup and pickle relish for a lunch treat |
| *CORN BREAD* | Use the packaged variety as an alternate for biscuits |
| *LEFTOVERS* | See "Chinese Fried Rice" in Appendix B and adapt as needed. In a fry pan, melt some oleo, crack in one egg and stir, then stir fry any fresh or canned veggies, meats or fish with a chopped onion, and some soy sauce. Add a half cup of white wine, simmer until most of the liquid is gone and either serve over rice or add the cooked rice prior to adding the white wine. Great! |
| *BERRIES* | Get some canned varieties to alternate with the canned or fresh fruit on pancakes or cereals for breakfast. Also use as toppings on dessert cakes. |
| *CHILE CON CARNE OR BOSTON BAKED BEANS* | In lieu of pork and beans. Again, supplement with a bit of molasses and/or some brown sugar or syrup, perhaps a sautéed chopped onion and some dry mustard. |

**FREEZE-DRIED MEATS**    Obtain in any camping or back packing outlet. When ready to use, cover with warm water to reconstitute before adding to a combined dish such as stroganoff, chinese fried rice, canned beans, etc.

**GRANOLA**    In addition to packaged cold cereals.

**POTATO SIDE DISHES**    Found on your grocer's shelf. Substitute reconstituted dry milk for fresh and you will have several varieties from which to choose.

## *APPENDIX B*
### *RECIPES IN TWO PARTS*

*An explanation of abbreviations and other things along the way*

As in Appendix A, those *"TIPS"* you come across are for you, Mate.

c. = cup

uppercase <u>T</u>.= tablespoon   lowercase <u>t</u>. = teaspoon

The word "can" is spelled out so as not to get confused with the "c." meaning "cup."

### *PART 1: THE HAWAII RACE MENUS, APPENDIX A*

(As I said before, you will not need most of these simple read-off-the-box directions. But I did promise to list the recipes, and maybe you will pick up an idea or two. My apologies in advance if what follows seems a return to Middle School White Sauce 101!)

The recipes appear in the order in which they are referenced in the race menus (Appendix A).

### *Orange Juice Mixture*

*For a half-gallon pitcher*

Using Tang© and Wyler's® lemonade mix, mix 3 scoops of each (the large measuring scoop that comes with the can) into pitcher; fill with cold water and stir.

*TIP: One or two large containers of each dry mix is plenty for an extended cruise. These sure beat the storage space needed for the bottled or canned variety, and the frozen concentrates are only good for the first couple of days (unless, of course, you have a freezer).*

### Drop Biscuits

*TIP: Enough for 2 or 3 biscuits each for 7 crew members. Adjust amounts as needed for your crew.)*

2 c. Bisquick®

$\frac{2}{3}$ c. milk (use water if preferred)

Mix with fork. Lightly grease (or use Pam® spray) 2 cake pans, drop batter by teaspoonful, leaving space between drops. Bake approx. 10 minutes at 450°.

### Regular Flapjacks/Hot Cakes

*(Serves 7 people. For 2 to 5, use amounts shown in parentheses ().*

3 c. (2) Krusteaz© pancake mix

$1\frac{1}{2}$ c. (1) water

Mix, let stand a few minutes, add more water if necessary to get desired consistency. Cook in normal manner in greased fry pan. Keep warm in oven.

*TIP #1: Personally I think Krusteaz© is the best ready-to-make pancake mix available in that it requires water, not milk, and the mixture actually becomes "yeasty"; the hot cakes rise like yeast rolls if the humidity cooperates, that is. Sooo good.*

*TIP #2: To avoid greasy pancakes, melt a glob of oleo in fry pan; when it has melted, wipe up excess with a couple of paper towels. After each batch, re-wipe the skillet with the "oleo-ed" paper towel. During cooking, park that soggy towel on a paper plate.*

### Beer Pancackes

Same as above, but substitute stale beer for half the water.

### Special Hot Oatmenal

*Serves 6 at a time; increase or decrease as necessary*

Bring 2 c. water to a boil. Sprinkle with either cinnamon or nutmeg, or a touch of both. Omit salt.

Add 1 c. one-minute quick cooking-type oatmeal, a handful of raisins, some crushed nut topping and a spoonful or so of brown sugar.

Stir while boiling for one minute. Cover and remove from heat. Serve in 5 minutes with more brown sugar on top.

### Chinese Fried Rice

*Serves 6-10 easily*

Cook 2 c. instant rice according to directions, but add 2 bouillon cubes to the cooking water and substitute white wine for half the water.

Sauté a chopped onion in oleo; stir in a raw egg. If any zucchini left, cut it up and add. Add cooked rice and about $\frac{1}{3}$ c. soy sauce and $\frac{1}{2}$ c. water and wine combined. Cook until most of the liquid is gone and the rice is nice and brown.

### Pudding Tip

*Garnish with shredded coconut and/or cake sprinkles.*

### Clams and Linguine

*Serves 8 to 10 normal appetites. For 2 or 3, use 1 can of clams and amend the rest of the ingredients accordingly by a fourth.*

4 cans minced clams with liquid (7 oz. each)

4 or 5 T. oleo

1 t. garlic powder or 1½ t. garlic "sprinkle"

2-3 t. dry spaghetti sauce mix

1 c. white wine

1 package of linguine (or "Angel Hair" if preferred)

Boiling water

4 t. parsley flakes

Parmesan cheese

*Melt oleo in sauce pan. Add clams with liquid. Stir in garlic powder (sprinkles) and spaghetti sauce mix. Add wine and simmer uncovered until liquid is reduced by at least one half, about a half hour.*

*Meanwhile, cook pasta in boiling water till done. Drain and rinse. Put on plates, sprinkle with parsley flakes. Pour over the clam sauce and top with cheese. Or let everyone do their own plate, serving the pasta on a platter and the sauce in a pot with a ladle. Cheese on the side.*

## Beer Bread

*Makes two loaves. Think 4-3-1, this is so easy!*

4 c. Bisquick®

3 T. sugar

1 12-oz. can beer

*Mix all together in large bowl. Grease 2 small loaf pans. Divide dough between. Let rise 10 minutes. Bake @ 375° for 30 minutes.*

*THAT'S IT!*

## *PART 2: FOOD FOR ADDITIONAL THOUGHT AND GOOD MEASURE*

### *These are listed according to categories.*

### *APPETIZERS*

#### **Sashimi Appetizer**

Using the fish you catch in untainted waters, marinate thin raw slices of filleted fish in a bowl with $\frac{1}{4}$ c. each of lemon juice, soy sauce and teriyaki sauce. Add a chopped onion and either chopped fresh celery or dried celery flakes and let stand for a couple of hours. Serve with crackers.

#### **Marinated Mushrooms**

Marinate one 10 oz. can of button mushrooms in:

$\frac{1}{3}$ c. wine vinegar

$\frac{1}{3}$ c. olive oil

$\frac{1}{2}$ t. onion salt

$\frac{1}{4}$ t. celery salt

$\frac{1}{4}$ t. marjoram

1 t. parsley flakes

Cover and chill for at least 4 hours. These will keep under refrigeration for several days. If no refrigeration, either eat hearty or invite more boaters over for a raft-up.

### DINNER TIME!!

## Old-Fashioned Corn Chowder

*Serves 2 or 3*

1 onion, chopped

3 slices salt pork (or canned bacon), cubed

4 potatoes, sliced thin

1 can corn, creamed style

Milk (use powdered to make approx 1 pint)

Salt and pepper to taste.

*Sauté onion and salt pork (or bacon) until light brown. Add just enough water to boil the potatoes. When done, add corn, milk and seasonings and continue to heat on low flame until everything is heated to "hot" and ready to eat.*

## Far-Out Eggplant

*Serves 4 to 6*

1 eggplant, sliced and peeled

2 zucchini, sliced

1 can tomato sauce, 8 oz. size

1 T. soy sauce

$\frac{3}{4}$ c. green pepper, chopped, or 2 T. dehydrated pepper or vegetable flakes

1 can mushrooms, 8 oz. size, drained

Cheese, about $\frac{3}{4}$ c. or so, cut into cubes

1 c. water

Parmesan cheese

*Sauté peppers and mushrooms in oleo or butter. Simmer the eggplant and zucchini in approx $1/4$ c. of water combined with the soy sauce until no longer raw but not too soft, either. Transfer half of the eggplant mixture to a casserole dish, top with half the tomato sauce and pepper mixture, distribute half the cubed cheese. Repeat layers and sprinkle the top with Parmesan cheese. Bake at 350° for 20-30 minutes.*

### Seafarin' Cabbage Rolls

*Serves 4 to 6*

1 head of green cabbage

1 can corned beef hash, 15 oz. size

1 onion, chopped

1 egg (or use powdered or substitute type)

Worcestershire sauce

Oleo or butter

Honey

*Parboil cabbage for 5 minutes; cut out the core. Combine the hash, onion, egg, a dash of Worcestershire. Using 3 leaves of cabbage per serving, make 3-leaf "nests" and spoon a good-sized portion of the hash mixture into each. Tuck in ends and wrap.*

*Put in a baking dish seam side down. Dot each one with oleo or butter and a teaspoon or so of honey. Bake at 325° for an hour, turning once.*

### Rummed Ham

*Serves 2 to 8*

1 canned ham, 2 to 5 pound size

$\frac{1}{4}$ c. to $\frac{1}{2}$ c. jar orange marmalade, depending on size of ham

$\frac{1}{2}$ c. rum

$\frac{1}{2}$ to 1 can green beans, drained

*Cover ham with marmalade and rum; bake approx. one hour at 350°. Put green beans around the ham and return to oven.*

*When beans are hot through, serve with instant mashed potatoes and canned fruit.*

### Rice and Beef

*Serves 2 to 4*

1 can mushroom soup

1 can tomato soup

1 large jar dried beef, cut in small pieces or shredded

1 can peas (not drained)

$\frac{1}{4}$ t. each pepper, celery salt, and oregano

1 to 2 t. hot sauce (*very* optional!)

*Add everything to a large fry pan; heat to a boil then simmer for 10 minutes. Add enough water to make a sauce.*

*Serve over rice.*

## Clam Chowder

*Serves 4 to 6*

1 can clam chowder

1 can cream of potato soup

1 can minced clams with juice

3 soup cans of milk (use powdered and mixed)

Fish…canned (and flaked) as much as possible

*Season to taste: thyme, basil, parsley flakes, pimento, dill weed, salt and pepper (or lemon pepper).*

*If you have fresh fish, use instead of the canned, of course. Add cooked crab, shrimp, lobster, whatever is on hand. Serve with corn bread, rolls or biscuits, and a salad.*

## Chicken Chow Mein, Simplified

*Serves 4*

1 can chow mein vegetables

1 can cream of mushroom soup

2 cans boned chicken, cut into cubes

1 can chow mein noodles

*Mix and heat first 3 ingredients. Serve over the noodles.*

## Corned Beef Casserole

*Serves 3 to 4*

1 can corned beef

1 can cream of celery soup

1 t. salt

2 T. onion powder

2 T. parsley flakes

$\frac{1}{2}$ c. water

1 package macaroni and cheese

*Cook macaroni, drain, and add the rest of the ingredients and reheat.*

## Mussel Bisque

*If you are lucky enough to snare yourself a bunch of mussels, try this one. In a large pot, place:*

$\frac{1}{2}$ c. sherry
$\frac{1}{2}$ whole onion
Parsley flakes
1 t. paprika
2 cloves whole garlic
Salt and pepper
1 can cream of mushroom soup
And the mussels of course…about 3 quarts
        if you can swing it.

*In a separate pot, heat soup. Steam the mussels till they open. Remove the whole mussels with a slotted spoon and keep warm. Strain the mussel broth and whisk it into the mushroom soup. Place mussels, in their shells, in large soup bowls and pour the broth over them. Serve with garlic toast.*

### Slumgullion

*This is for the end of the line when you are just about out of everything, including ideas. It will keep your reputation as an Improvising Cook Extraordinaire alive and well and living on the high seas. Should serve 4.*

1 can kidney beans with sauce

1 can Mexican hot sauce, 7 oz. size

2 bouillon cubes (chicken if using chicken or fish, beef if using freeze-dried meats, canned meat, etc.)

*Gather unto you any and all pieces of chicken or meat or fish that you can find. Simmer the whole thing for 15 minutes. Accompany with ice cold vodka and water.*

*A sure winner, mate. Especially with the vodka.*

### Rum Baked Beans

*This one serves 6. Recipe easy to halve for fewer appetites.*

2 cans beans, 20 oz. size

3 slices canned pineapple

1 clove garlic, minced

$\frac{1}{4}$ c. rum

$\frac{1}{4}$ c. soy sauce

$\frac{1}{4}$ c. honey

*Empty beans into a casserole; mix in everything else except the pineapple. Top with pineapple slices and bake uncovered at 350° for 45-50 minutes. Grreat!!*

### *MORE CRUISING BREADS*

**These require no perishable ingredients and are simple to do.**

### Casserole Bread (White)

2 c. warm water

1 T. dry yeast

2 t. salt

1 T. sugar

4 c. white flour, preferably unbleached

*Dissolve salt and sugar in water; add yeast. After 5 minutes, add flour. Dough will be sticky. Let rise till double in size. Stir down and divide between 2 well-greased small loaf pans. Sprinkle top with salt and let rise again until double. Bake approx 45-60 minutes at 375°. Allow to cool in pan for 10 minutes, then remove and cool completely.*

*This is the basic recipe. If you like garlic, add 3 shakes or so of garlic powder. Dried minced onions (about 2 T.) make onion bread (add the onion to the yeast water to rehydrate).*

*One tablespoon of dill weed or basil or oregano gives three further variations.*

### No-Knead Whole Wheat Bread

2 c. warm water

1 T. dry yeast

1 T. honey

2 T. molasses

1 T. salt

3$\frac{1}{2}$ to 4 c. whole wheat flour

*Put honey and molasses in warm water; add yeast and allow to work for 5 to 10 minutes. Mix salt and flour, add to the yeast mixture. Stirring as vigorously as you can and starting with 3 $\frac{1}{2}$ c., gradually add mixture including the last $\frac{1}{2}$ c. if necessary.*

*Again, the dough will be sticky. Put into 2 small well-greased loaf pans; the pans should be about half full. Let rise to top of pans and bake at 350° for 45-60 minutes or until crust is dark brown and center tests done with a whisk broom straw (clean!) or a knife. Brush top with oil, butter or oleo and cool for 10 minutes. Loosen from sides, remove from pans and cool upside down for another 20 minutes (**If** you can keep the crew away, that is! The aroma that you have just created will drive 'em right up the mast!)*

*Variations can be done with the addition of other flours such as rye, barley or buckwheat. Start by substituting a cup of the alternate flour for a cup of the whole wheat. Also, try adding $\frac{1}{2}$ c. of sesame seeds for a nutty flavor.*

## A TODDY FOR THE BODY

Rainy Day Pick-Me-Ups: Make these in advance if possible, and store in empty instant coffee jars. Using 2 **rounded** teaspoons per cup of water (unless otherwise noted), each recipe yields 20 cups, again except where noted.

### Suisse Mocha

$\frac{1}{2}$ c. instant coffee    $\frac{1}{2}$ c. sugar    1 c. nonfat dry milk

2 T. unsweetened cocoa    $\frac{1}{8}$ t. baking powder

*Mix well.*

### Café Vienna

$\frac{1}{2}$ c. instant coffee    $\frac{2}{3}$ c. sugar    $\frac{2}{3}$ c. nonfat dry milk

$\frac{1}{2}$ t. cinnamon    $\frac{1}{8}$ t. baking powder

*Blend ingredients well.*

### Café Capuccino

$\frac{1}{2}$ c. instant coffee  $\frac{3}{4}$ c. sugar  1 c. nonfat dry milk

$\frac{1}{2}$ t. dried orange peel  $\frac{1}{8}$ t. baking soda

*Crush orange peel with a spoon to release the essence. Mix well with other ingredients.*

**"It's a naive domestic burgundy, without any breeding, but I think you'll be amused by its presumption.""**
**— James Thurber, cartoon caption**

### Russian Tea

2 c. sugar   $\frac{1}{2}$ c. instant tea   2 c. Tang©

1 t. cinnamon   $\frac{1}{2}$ t. ground cloves

*Mix together. Use 3 heaping t. in 1 c. water.*

### Italian Mocha Espresso

1 c. instant coffee  1 c. sugar

$4\frac{1}{2}$ c. nonfat dry milk   $\frac{1}{2}$ c. cocoa  $\frac{1}{2}$ t. baking soda.

*Mix well. Use 2 t. in $\frac{1}{2}$ c.of water. Yields 36 cups.*

## SIDELIGHTS

### Far-Out/Far East Salad Dressing

$\frac{1}{2}$ c. catsup

2 T. mayo

$\frac{1}{4}$ c. soy sauce

$\frac{1}{4}$ c. teriyaki sauce or saki

1 t. powdered ginger

2 t. lemon juice

*Combine all ingredients. Serve over cabbage or lettuce salads.*

*APPENDIX C:*
*FOOD/SUPPLY INVENTORY LISTS:*
*BY LOCATION—SEE DIAGRAM OF*
*LAYOUT*

## GALLEY

### A

Dishes
Platters
Dish bowls
Soup bowls, extra
Serving bowls (microwave oven casserole)

### B

Bisquick®
Flour, all purpose
Pancake mix
Potato dish, instant, mashed
Raisins
Rice, instant
Sugar, white
Sugar, brown
Sugar substitutes

### C

Cereals, hot
Cereals, cold
36 pkgs. milk, instant, dry, ea. 1 qt.

### D

Crackers
Peanut butter
Honey
Jam
Wyler's®(dry lemonade mix)
Tang©(dry orange drink mix)
Rye Krisp®

### E

Blender top
Coffee, instant
Cocoa, non instant
Cocoa, instant (Nestlé Quik®)
Creamer, coffee
Egg beater
Malted milk, instant
Wooden spoons, extra

### F

Coffee, regular
Coffee pot and filters
Hot chocolate, individual pkgs.
Tea bags

### G

#### ALL SPICES

Baking soda
Baking powder
Basil
Bay leaves, whole
Bell pepper flakes
Bouillon cubes
Celery salt
Chili powder
Cinnamon, ground
Cinnamon, stick
Cloves, ground
Curry powder
Dill weed

Flour, Wondra® shaker container
Garlic, fresh
Garlic powder
Ginger, ground
Hickory salt
Horseradish, prepared
Ketchup
Kikkoman© sauce
Lemon pepper
Molasses
Mustard, ground
Nutmeg
Onion, dehydrated minced
Oregano
Paprika
Parsley flakes
Pepper, ground—black
Pepper, whole—black
Pepper, seasoned
Salt, seasoned
Thyme, ground
Soy sauce
Teriyaki sauce
Vegetable cooking spray, Pam©
Vanilla flavoring

## H

Croutons
Sunflower Seeds
Pickles
Salad Oil
Shortening (lard)
Vinegars for salads
Salad dressings, bottled
Syrup

### GALLEY UNDER SINK

Rice, regular to put in salt (helps offset humidity complications)

All cleaning supplies (except oven and rug cleaners)

### GALLEY UNDER OVEN

Cake pans      Bread pans      Baking pans

### GALLEY NOTES

Pots 'n' pans—General in small hold under microwave. Includes blender, vegetable steamer, etc

Large stew/soup/spaghetti pot, large mixing bowls in cupboard under cutlery drawer

### AFT HEAD

Bleach, 1 large
Baking soda for cleaning only, 1 large
Plastic glasses, 4 pkgs. (18 in ea.) shower ceiling head
Toilet paper, 4 rolls
Vegetable oil, 1 extra
Fresh produce, extra in shower
Beer in shower

### FORWARD HEAD

Bleach, 1 large
Dental Kit (minimal supplies: all crew members should bring their own), 1
Di-Gel®, 1
First aid kit, 1 (basic with baking soda)
Salt tablets, approx. 100
Toilet paper, 4 rolls

### AFT STATEROOM

Aluminum foil, 1 roll, 200 sq. ft.
Flatware, plastic picnic-type, assorted
Garbage bags, 1/2 box white, 2"x2"x6"
Plastic wrap, generic, 1 roll, 300 sq. ft.△
Plastic wrap, Handi-Wrap®, 1 roll, 125 sq. ft.△
Cheese, bulk extra supply
Kitchen towels
Toaster
Paper plates and napkins, extra
    △Use supply on engine room door *first*

## MAIN SALON

### BAR

Drawer below: jars of olives, onions, bottle opener, can opener, etc.

### CUPBOARD #1 CANNED GOODS

Extra can opener

#### JUICES (all cans are 46 oz.)

| | | |
|---|---|---|
| 1 Tomato | 1 V-8® | 1 Pineapple |
| 2 Apple | 1 Grapefruit | |

#### VEGETABLES

3 Corn, whole kernel, 16oz.
2 Mixed, large cut, 29oz.
1 Lima beans, 17oz.
1 Beets, shoestring, 16oz.
1 Zucchini, 16oz.
2 Peas, 17oz.

#### FRUIT

4 Pears, halves, 29oz.
3 Fruit cocktail, 30oz.
2 Peaches, sliced, 29oz.
2 Pineapple, sliced, 20oz.

#### MEALS/MEAL SUPPLEMENTS

5 Hash, roast beef, 15oz.
1 Hash, corned beef, 24oz.
1 Tuna, chunk, 12oz.
2 Clams, chopped, 7oz.
1 Refried beans, 16oz.
3 Pork and beans, 30oz.
1 Clams, whole, 16oz.

### SOUPS/CANNED

All 11 oz. To be used for sauces except where noted
2 Consommé   6 Cream of mushroom
1 Tomato      1 Cheddar cheese
1 Clam chowder (Chef's choice item) ea. 15oz.

### MISCELLANEOUS

2 Cranberry sauce, whole, 16oz.
2 Cranberry sauce, jellied, 16oz.

### CUPBOARD 1A (Triangle)

Excess supply cupboard. Racers should not need these supplies *(Note: Turned out that they did!)*
1 Ketchup, 32oz.
1 Coffee creamer, 22oz.
1 Pam© vegetable spray, 12oz.
2 Pancake/Waffle mix, 2 lb. box.
1 Pancake mix, Krusteaz©, 7 lb. bag.
2 Shake 'n' Bake® Twin Pak/Chicken, ea. 7oz.
1 Shake 'n' Bake® Single/Chicken, 7oz.
1 Syrup, 36 oz.
1 Instant brkfst. mix, asst. flavors, 24 pkgs.

### CUPBOARD #2

1 Peanut butter, 18oz.
1 Milk, evaporated, 13oz.
2 Milk, evaporated, 5.3oz.
1 Mayonnaise, 32oz.
2 Relish, sweet, 22oz.
2 Spaghetti sauce, 32oz.
1 Salsa, 12oz.
2 Applesauce (for ham), 15oz.
2 Hams, canned, ea. 5 lb.
2 Bacon, canned, ea. 16oz.
1 Salad vinegar, 24oz.
1 Salad dressing, Thousand Island, 16oz.
1 Coffee, regular, 3 lb.
2 Brown bread, canned, ea. 16oz.

### Canned tomato products

2 peeled tomatoes, 28oz.
2 peeled tomatoes, 16oz.
3 tomato sauce, 15oz.
1 tomato sauce, 8oz.
1 tomato paste, 12oz.
**Day bags for** *day #2 only*

### CUPBOARD #3

All other day bags

### CUPBOARD #4

4 Coffee cake mix—use 2 ea for B-4 & B-11
1 Bisquick®, 60oz.
2 pkgs. noodles, wide, 12oz.
2 pkgs. noodles, narrow, 12oz.
2 pkgs. spaghetti, raw, 16oz.
1 box potatoes au gratin, 11oz.
1 box potatoes, scalloped/2-3 servings, 5.6oz.
4 bags potato chips, large twin
1 stuffing mix (for D-9), 12oz.
2 boxes crackers, wheat, 10oz.
1 box crackers, garlic rounds, 6oz.
2 boxes rice, instant, ea 28oz.

### CUPBOARD #5

2 jars bouillon cubes, chicken and beef
1 coffee creamer, 11oz.
1 coffee, instant—decaf, 8oz.
1 cereal, hot—Cream of Wheat®, 28oz.
2 cereal, cold/assorted variety, 10 individ.
1 cornstarch, 16oz.
1 pkg. flour, all purpose, 5 lb.
1 cheese, dry grated, 8oz.
1 Wylers®lemonade mix,use w/Tang©, 30oz.
6 milk, dry lowfat, individ. pkgs, ea. pkg=1qt.
2 boxes muffin mix, bran, 9.75oz.
4 boxes muffin mix, bran/use 2 at a time, 7oz.

1 oatmeal, 1 minute quick cooking, 42oz.
1 bag Krusteaz pancake mix, 7lb.
2 pkgs. peanuts w/shells, 12oz.
1 salt, 26oz.
1 sugar, powdered, 16oz.
3 Tang© breakfast orange drink, 9 qts. total, 40.5oz.
3 pkgs. granola bars, assorted flavors

### 5 salad dressing mixes:

2 Buttermilk     2 French     1 Italian

### 15 sauces for gravy and meat supplements:

2 Pork   1 Stroganoff   3 Chicken   1 Stew
2 Taco   1 Enchilada   2 Burrito   3 Sloppy Joe

### 13 sauces, misc:

4 sour cream,     4 hollandaise,   5 hot dip
    for vegetables, etc.

### CUPBOARD #5A (DESSERTS)

### All Party supplies

1 bag marshmallows, large, 1 lb.
1 pkg. bake cups, total in package: 85.
2 pkgs. coconut flakes, 7oz.
1 can frosting mix, vanilla, 16.5oz.
paper plates, small—white, 50 ea. 2 pkg.
napkins cocktail size—white, 50 ea. 1 pkg.
napkins, birthday, 25 ea. 1 pkg.
chopsticks, 17 pr.

### Cake decorating supplies

1 tube red icing with 4 tops
1 jar sprinkles, decor., mixed
2 jars sprinkles, decor., chocolate
2.5 pkgs. cake candles, 40 total

### *Desserts*

3 Dream Whip®, dry
2 boxes cookies,
    1 oatmeal, 1 peanut butter
1 box carrot cake mix
1 box brownie mix
2 pkgs. Cheesecake (with crumbs in
    Ziploc®)
4 Jiffy Pop® popcorn containers
16 Pudding Mixes:  <u>Note:</u> ea box = 3+oz,
    or 3 to 4 servings.    7 people = 2 boxes
    2 <u>non</u> instant:      both  butterscotch
    14    instant:      4 banana
                     3 vanilla
                     3 pistachio
                     4 chocolate fudge

## *CUPBOARD #5B*

### *Paper Goods*

2 pkgs. napkins, family size
4 rolls paper towels
500 matches

### *Night Watch Supplies*

15 individual night bags, each bag includes
    7 servings of every item

## *STEP STORAGE 5C*

Oven cleaner
Rug cleaner
Insect sprays et al

# *NOTES*

## *ALPHABETICALLY BY ITEM—SEE DIAGRAM OF LAYOUT*

### A

| | |
|---|---|
| Apples | Hammock/aft shower |
| Aluminum foil | Engine room door/ aft stateroom |
| Apple juice | #1 |
| Applesauce | #2 |
| Au gratin potatoes | #4 |

### B

| | |
|---|---|
| Bacon, canned | #2 |
| Bake cups (muffin tin liners) | #5A |
| Baking soda | Galley G/fwd head/ aft head |
| Baking powder | Galley G |
| Basil | See Spices |
| Bay leaves | See Spices |
| Bell pepper flakes | See Spices |
| Beets, shoestring, canned | #1 |
| Bisquick® | Galley B/#4 |
| Bleach | Both heads |
| Blender, small | Pots/pan cupboard |
| Bran muffin mix | #5 |
| Bouillon cubes | Galley G and #5 |
| Bottle opener | Bar |
| Bread pans | Galley, under oven |
| Breakfast juices/drink | Galley D/#5 |
| Butter | Frig |

### C

| | |
|---|---|
| Cabbages | Hammock/aft shower under sink |
| Cake mixes | #5A |
| Cake decorating supplies | #5A |
| Can openers (4 ) | Galley cutlery drawer; #1; emergency stores; bar |
| Catsup | Galley G/1A |
| Cantaloupes | See Melons |
| Celery salt | See Spices |

| | |
|---|---|
| Cereals, hot and cold | Galley C/#5 |
| Cheddar cheese soup | #1 |
| Cheesecakes | #5A |
| Cheeses | Frig/aft stateroom |
| Cheese cutter | Galley drawer |
| Cheesecloth | Main cabin, lower port near Nav station |
| Chinese dinner  #3 (use both to serve 7, D-12) | |
| Cinnamon(s) | See Spices |
| Clam chowder, canned | #1 |
| Clams, chopped, canned | #1 |
| Cleaning supplies | Under Galley sink for oven or rug cleansers see "O" and "R" respectively) |
| Cloves | See Spices |
| Cocoa, non-instant | Galley E |
| Cocoa, instant (Nestlé Quik®) | Galley E |
| Coffee, instant (reg & decaf) | Galley E/#5 |
| Coffee, regular | Galley F/#2 |
| Coffee pot with filters | Galley F |
| Coffee cake mix | #4 |
| Consommé soup, canned | #1 |
| Cookie mixes | #5A |
| Cooking spray | See Pam© |
| Corn, whole kernel, canned | #1 |
| Cornflakes | Galley C/#5 |
| Cornstarch | #5 |
| Corkscrews | Bar |
| Crackers | Galley D/#4 |
| Cranberry Sauce, canned | #1 |
| Creamer, coffee | Galley E/#5 |
| Cream of mushroom soup | #1 |
| Croutons | Galley H |
| Curry powder | See Spices |
| Cutlery, table | Drawer under Galley sink |
| Cutlery, cooking | Galley E/ Lg cutlery drawer |

### D

| | |
|---|---|
| Dairy goods | Refrigerator |
| Dental kit (minimal) | Forward head |

Desserts, all #5A
Di-Gel® tablets Forward head
Dill weed See Spices
Dip sauce mix #5
Dishes Galley A
Dream Whip® #5A

### E

Eggs Frig under shelf
Egg beater Galley E

### F

First aid kit, basic Forward head
Flatware, table See Cutlery
Flour, all purpose Galley B/#5
Flour, Wondra® shaker container Galley G

### G

Garbage bags, paper Engine room
Garbage bags, plastic Aft stateroom
Garlic, fresh See Spices
Garlic powder See Spices
Ginger See Spices
Glasses, plastic See Plastic
Granola Galley C
Granola bars #5
Grapefruit juice #1
Gravy mixes #5
Grapefruits, fresh Hammock/aft shower
Grated cheese, dry #5

### H

Hams, canned #2
Hash, canned #1
Hickory salt See Spices
High energy food—night watch *only* #5B
Hollandaise sauce mix #5
Honey Galley D
Horseradish, prepared See Spices
Hot chocolate, individual pkgs Galley F

### I

Insect sprays (non-human)
Step Storage #5C
Instant mashed potatoes Galley B
Instant breakfast #1A
Instant soup mixes Day bags

### J

Jams Frig/Galley D
Juices, canned and bottled #1

### K

Kikkoman Sauce© See Spices

### L

Lard See Shortening
Lemonade mix Galley D/#5
Lemon pepper See Spices
Lima beans, canned #1

### M

Malted milk Galley E
Margarine See Oleomargerine
Marshmallows #5A
Matches #5B
Mayonnaise Frig/#2
Melons, cantaloupe Hammock/
aft shower under sink
Milk, canned #2
Milk, dry Galley C
Mixed vegetables, canned #1
Molasses Galley G
Muffin mix, bran #5
Mustard See Spices
Mustard sauce #2

### N

Napkins #5B/aft stateroom
Nestlé Quik® See Cocoa
Night watch high energy food #5B
Noodles, egg, all sizes #4
Nutmeg See Spices

## O

| | |
|---|---|
| Oatmeal, 1 min. quick cook | Galley C/#5 |
| Oleomargarine | Frig in the back |
| Onions, minced dried | See Spices |
| Onions, fresh | Hammock |
| Orange juice drink/dry | See Tang© |
| Oranges | Hammock/aft shower |
| Oregano | See Spices |
| Oven cleaner | Step Storage #5C |

## P

| | |
|---|---|
| Pancake mix | Galley B/#5 /#1A |
| Pam© cooking spray | Galley G/#1A |
| Paper bags | See Garbage bags |
| Paper towels | #5B |
| Paper plates | Aft stateroom |
| Paprika | See Spices |
| Parsley flakes | See Spices |
| Party supplies | #5A/ bar |
| Pasta (noodles, raw spaghetti, etc) | #4 |
| Peanuts, with shells (for *daytime* snacks) | #5 |
| Peaches, canned sliced | #1 |
| Peanut butter | Galley D/#2 |
| Pears, canned halves | #1 |
| Pepper, all kinds | See Spices |
| Pickle relish | Frig/#2 |
| Pickles | Galley H |
| Pineapple juice | See Juices |
| Pineapple, canned slices | #1 |
| Plastic glasses, small | Bar |
| Plastic glasses, large | Aft head in shower |
| Plastic forks, spoons, etc | Aft stateroom |
| Plastic wrap | Eng room door/aft stateroom |
| Popcorn | #5A |
| Pork and beans, canned | #1 |
| Potatoes, baking | 7 in hammock/ 7 in aft shower |
| Potatoes, instant | Galley B |
| Potatoes, scalloped | #4 |
| Potato chips | #4 |

| | |
|---|---|
| Pots and pans | See Galley notes |
| Pudding mixes | #5A |

## Q-R

| | |
|---|---|
| Raisins | Galley B |
| Refried beans, canned | #1 |
| Relish, sweet | Frig/#2 |
| Rice, instant | #4 |
| Rice, regular *(to put in salt container for humidity)* | Galley under sink |
| Rug cleaner | Step storage #5C |
| Rye Krisp® | Galley D |

## S

| | |
|---|---|
| Salad dressing, bottled | Galley H/#2 |
| Salad dressing, mixes | #5 |
| Salad oil | See Vegetable oil |
| Salad vinegars | Galley H/#2 |
| Salsa | #2 |
| Salt, regular, iodized (table use) | Table shaker/#5 |
| Salt, regular (housekeeping) | Galley under sink |
| Salt, seasoned | See Spices |
| Salt tablets | Forward head |
| Saltine crackers | See Crackers |
| Sauce mixes | #5 |
| Scalloped potato mix | #4 |
| Shake 'N' Bake® | #1A |
| Shortening (lard) | Galley H |
| Soda pop | Main salon, lower port near Nav station |
| Soups, canned | #1 |
| Soup mixes, dry, e.g., Top Ramen© | Day bags in #2 & #3 |
| Sour cream mix | #5 |
| Soy sauce | Galley G |
| Spaghetti noodles | #4 |
| Spaghetti sauce, prepared | #2 |
| Spices, all | Galley G |
| Stuffing mix for D-9 | #4 |

| | |
|---|---|
| Sugar, brown | Galley B |
| Sugar, powdered | #5 |
| Sugar, regular | Galley B |
| Sugar substitutes | Galley B |
| Sunflower seeds for salads | Galley H |
| Syrup | Galley H/#1A |

### T

| | |
|---|---|
| Tang© breakfast drink | Galley D/#5 |
| Tea bags | Galley F |
| Teriyaki sauce | Galley G |
| Thyme | See Spices |
| Toilet paper | Both heads |
| Towels, kitchen | Aft stateroom |
| Toaster | Aft stateroom |
| Tomato juice | See Juices |
| Tomatoes, canned and peeled | #2 |
| Tomato sauce | #2 |
| Tomato paste | #2 |
| Tomato soup | #1 |
| Tuna fish, canned | #1 |

### U-V

| | |
|---|---|
| Vanilla flavoring | Galley G |
| V-8® juice | See Juices |
| Vegetables, canned | #1 |
| Vegetable sauce mixes | #5 |
| Vegetable oil | Galley H/aft head under sink |
| Vinegar, salad | See Salad vinegars |
| Vinegar, white | Under Galley sink |

### W, X, Y, Z

| | |
|---|---|
| Wine vinegars | See Salad vinegars |
| Wooden spoons | Galley E/ lg cutlery drawer |
| Zucchini, canned | #1 |

### FREEZER PACK LIST

**NOTE: All packages of english muffins in lower frig.**

List given is from **bottom to top**

| | | |
|---|---|---|
| 1. | 1.5# uncooked hamburger meat | D-15 |
| 2. | 1 bag cut up baked chicken (20 pcs.)△ | D-13 |
| 3. | 1 lg. loaf whole wheat bread | L-12 |
| 4. | 1 pkg. bread sticks | D-11 |
| 5. | 2 bags beef (beer) stew△ | D-10 |
| 6. | 2 bags baked chicken pcs. 7 ea./bag△ | D-9 |
| 7. | 1 lg. loaf whole wheat bread | L-8 |
| 8. | 1 bag beef strognaoff△ | D-7 |
| 9. | 1 rnd. container, spaghetti sauce△ | D-6 |
| 10. | 1 bottle container, split pea soup△ | D-5 |
| 11. | 1 pkg. french bread | D-5 |
| 12. | 2 bags beef stew△ | D-4 |
| 13. | 2 pkgs. whole wheat bread | L-4 |
| 14. | 1 pkg. uncooked hamburger meat | D-3 |
| 15. | 1 pkg. french bread | D-2 |
| 16. | 1 pkg. french bread | D-1 |

△These are your pre-cooked meals.

Please check off all items
when removed from freezer.

# *MORE NOTES*

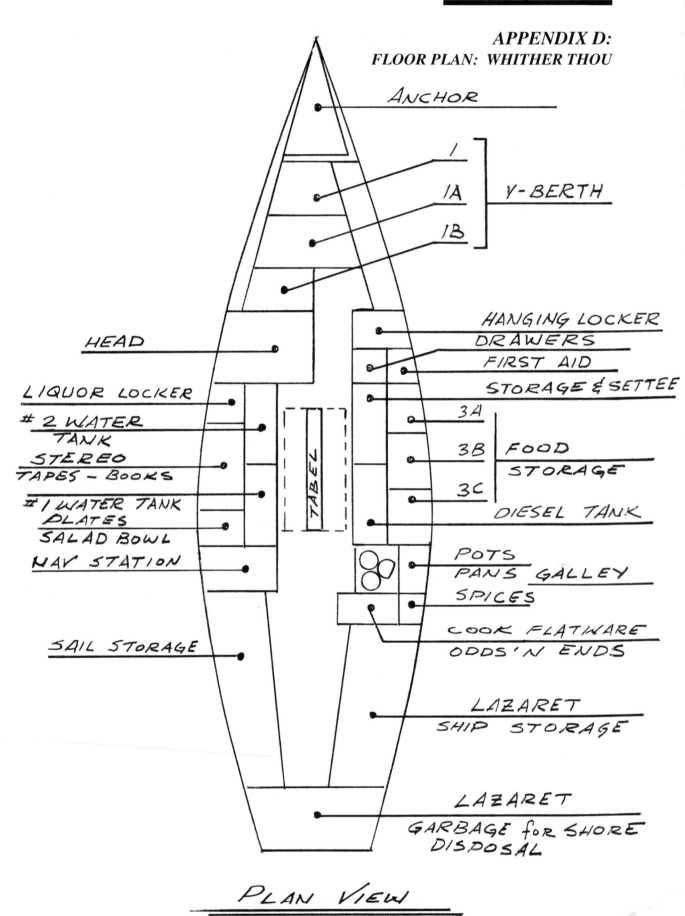

**APPENDIX D:**
**FLOOR PLAN: WHITHER THOU**

ANCHOR

1
1A — V-BERTH
1B

HEAD

HANGING LOCKER
DRAWERS
FIRST AID
STORAGE & SETTEE

LIQUOR LOCKER
#2 WATER TANK
STEREO
TAPES – BOOKS
#1 WATER TANK
PLATES
SALAD BOWL
NAV STATION

TABEL

3A
3B — FOOD
3C    STORAGE
DIESEL TANK

POTS
PANS — GALLEY
SPICES
COOK FLATWARE
ODDS'N ENDS

SAIL STORAGE

LAZARET
SHIP STORAGE

LAZARET
GARBAGE for SHORE
DISPOSAL

PLAN VIEW

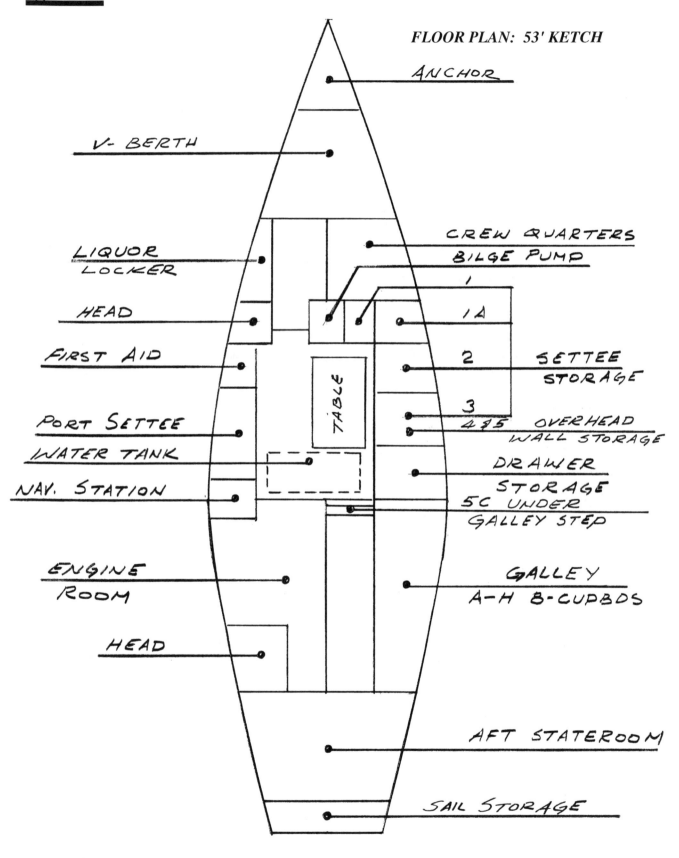

**FLOOR PLAN: 53' KETCH**

ANCHOR

V- BERTH

CREW QUARTERS

BILGE PUMP

LIQUOR
LOCKER

HEAD

1

1A

FIRST AID

2    SETTEE
     STORAGE

PORT SETTEE

3

4 & 5   OVERHEAD
        WALL STORAGE

WATER TANK

DRAWER

NAV. STATION

STORAGE
5C UNDER
GALLEY STEP

TABLE

ENGINE
ROOM

GALLEY
A-H  B-CUPBDS

HEAD

AFT STATEROOM

SAIL STORAGE

PLAN - VIEW

*APPENDIX E*

### *WHAT WORKED FOR ME MIGHT WORK FOR YOU!*

Gene Haynes


## 1. JURY RIGGING A LAZARET HINGE

When Dottie and I returned from Canada, I had several hinges seize, breaking as soon as the hatch was opened. The cruise schedule did not allow a repair stop nor could the budget be stretched for eight hinges in the name of uniformity. My answer was a plastic bottle that had once held a gallon of kerosene.

1) Cut a suitable size square out of either flat side. 6"x 8" is fine.

2) Trace the outline of the broken hinge on the square.

3) Drill or punch out the holes for the mounting hardware.

4) Cut out the new hinge with a knife or scissors and mount in place.

The plastic is extremely durable, bending as needed but at the same time providing the necessary stiffness to hold the lazaret cover securely in place. For extra strength, double the hinge and secure them together.

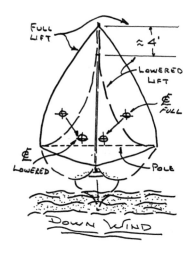

## 2. TWIN HEADSAILS: ALTERNATIVE TO THE SPINNAKER

Twin headsails, flown both as a spinnaker alternative or in their own right, could have an important place in your sail complement. If your crew is either a shorthanded one or singlehanded, twins could mean easier sailing, less effort and faster passages with graceful runs downwind.

I have personally sailed this configuration the whole "nine yards"—from my introduction to the concept via John Letcher's book on self-steering right through to my personal ultimate test…eight days in the tradewinds to Hawaii. Contrary to popular but misleading beliefs, my boat did not rock with this rig, nor did I experience a "spinnaker death roll." On the contrary, the twins proved themselves superior to the spinnaker in two ways.

Here's what I did; maybe it will work for you.

With my first boat, a 26' Columbia Mark I, I had two worn-out jibs restored and re-cut to 90%. On "Whither Thou" I initially borrowed a sister ship's 120% genoa and flew it with my own 130% one. Unfortunately, I was using the small jib pole which bent like a pretzel and exploded. Lesson: I upgraded to a 3" diameter/12' long one-piece spinnaker pole set with piston ends and topping lifts.

Eventually I went to my favorite sailmaker for a new system, comprised of a set of 150% genoas made of 1.5 oz. nylon. When I first flew them, another lesson was learned: "Whither" can rock given the right wind hit, but she was easily stabilized by bringing the mainsail into service.

Twin headsails have a smaller head than bloopers; therefore the mainsail blanks the head when opened for a run. However, since it is the purpose of the twins to balance the forward effort equally on both sides of the hull's horizontal center (thereby eliminating the unbalanced sail effort of wing-and-wing), it helps to reef the main once or twice, placing it in line with the hull's horizontal center. This gives the hull a "keel" in the air, thus increasing the stability.

Back to those eight days in Hawaiian tradewinds and the two advantages of twin headsails: Advantage #1: I set those twins for the total eight days and never once had to lower them: they need little attention; I literally flew them 24 hours a day.

Advantage #2: They are reefable. Yep, reefable. When I was approaching Kauai in the singlehanded race, it was blowing stink and my knotmeter had pegged out at 10 knots, although I knew I was doing at least 14. There I was, surfing at hull speed...I sure didn't want to put up a smaller sail and lose all the speed! Solution? I reefed. Picture it. By lowering the halyard 4' or so, the sails fall on the forestay, allowing each foot to form a beautiful "cup." The clew is held in place by the pole and its topping lift, but the head area of the sail gives way to the wind, reducing the overall area. The center of sail effort is lowered dramatically, reducing the drive effort, and the boat slows down to a sane speed.

To control the sail shape with the sheets, I found the extruded toe rail with its hole pattern gives the best choices of any angular adjustment you may wish to use. Hands-on practice will show you what these angles can do under different wind conditions.

I have also found I can broad reach up to 30° by offsetting the twins, but forget about long periods of beam reaching. This is where a reaching spinnaker, a blooper or your largest genoa comes into its own. If you need to beam reach for just a short period, lay one twin against the other and tie the clews together.

Unfortunately, not all hulls will react favorably to twins. Death rolls are something I have yet to experience, but try out your own hull. Find out for yourself whether it can handle the twin headsail rig. You may be in for a pleasant surprise.

Are twins as fast as spinnakers? Of course not. Spinnakers are, and will remain, the choice of racers with a crew of three or more. But for the lone sailor, or the cruising couple, twin headsails offer a gracious alternative.

## TWIN HEADSAILS SUGGESTIONS: A SUMMARY

1.  Set your mast facetrack with two separate pole blocks.

2.  Your pole length should be 80% of your "J" dimension, giving a good concave sail shape using a 150% genoa. Also you must be able to set those poles, so consider your physical size. Let topping lifts help as another mechanical advantage.

3.  Rig for both topping lifts to support both poles.

4.  Use a fixed length spinnaker pole with piston ends.

5.  Have your sail cut as a genoa, not as a fuller head blooper, etc.

6.  Don't go over 150%; a larger size needs too long a pole. (Also, if you race and your headsail exceeds 150%, your race handicap could suffer.)

7.  Your clew height should be cut about 4' to 6' above the deck. Set it with the tack on an extender approx. 18" to 24"; now your sail will not chafe or lie excessively on your pulpit or lifelines.

8.  Raise the twins on a single halyard. For testing purposes, you can always make a line adjuster on the tack for equal luff lengths.

9.  Sail with your main reefed and positioned in line with the hull. In calm waters, store it below.

10. Before investing, borrow a sail from a buddy and test your hull in a decent blow, say, 15-20 knots. But start your test slowly in winds of 5-10 knots.

11. For testing purposes, the sails need not be the same size; a 100% and a 130% work great.

12. You won't need two headstays. For bluewater cruising (or racing), go to the next largest diameter.

# *INDEX*

*BIBLIOGRAPHY*

*Webster's Ninth New Collegiate Dictionary.* Springfield, MA: Merriam-Webster, Inc.,
        1986.

Street, Donald. **The Ocean Sailing Yacht.** New York: W. W. Norton & Co., Inc.,      1973

Ross, Wallace with Chapman, C. *Sail Power.* New York: Alfred A. Knopf, 1977

Van Dorn, Wm. G. *Oceanography and Seamanship.* New York: Dodd Mead & Co.,
        1974

Henderson, R. *Singlehanded Sailing.* Camden, ME: Marine Publishing Co., 1976.

Letcher, John S. *Self Steering for Sailing Craft.* Camden, ME: International Publishing
        Co., 1974

Maté, Ferenc. *From a Bare Hull.* Vancouver, B.C., Canada: Albatross Publishing House,
        1977

Rawson and Miner, jt. comps. *New International Dictionary of Quotations.* New York:
        New American Library, 1986

-----------*New International Dictionary of Quotations,* 2nd ed. (A Dutton Book) New
        York: E. P. Dutton & Co., 1993

*God's in his heaven—*

*All's right with the world.*

*— Robert Browning*

# ORDER FORM

| QTY | TITLE | PRICE | CAN.PRICE | TOTAL |
|-----|-------|-------|-----------|-------|
| | *Provisioning—Bowsprit to Transom* <br> 208 pages | $19.95 | $26.95 | |
| | *But I Don't Want to Cook! Book* <br> 272 pages | 19.95 | 26.95 | |
| | Subtotal | | | |
| | Shipping and handling <br> (add $3.50 for one book, $1.00 for each additional book) | | | |
| | Sales tax (WA residents only, add 8%) | | | |
| | Total Enclosed | | | |

**Telephone Orders:**
Call 1-800-468-1994. Have your
VISA or Mastercard ready.

**Fax Orders:**
1-206-468-2399. Fill out order
blank and fax.

**Postal Orders:**
Goldberry Publishing
Route 2, Box 3028
Lopez, WA 98261

## Payment: Please Check One

❑ Check

❑ MasterCard

❑ VISA

**Exp. Date:**
_____ / _____

**Card Number** _____

**Name on Card** _____

NAME _____

ADDRESS _____

CITY _____

STATE _____ ZIP _____

DAYTIME PHONE _____

If this is a library book, please photocopy this page.
Quantity discounts are available. For more information, call 206-468-3019.

### *Thank you for your order!*
I understand that I may return any books
for a full refund if not satisfied.